W9-CFK-326

PUFFIN BOOKS

Editor : Kaye Webb

THE TALE OF TROY

This fine new telling of the tale of Troy covers the whole of that adventure which was the last of the great Greek heroes. '*It is in my mind,*' said *Zeus*, '*to cause the great and glorious war of Troy, that shall be famous to the end of time. Famous too shall be the names of the heroes who fight at Troy, but with them the Age of Heroes shall end, and the Iron Age of ordinary men shall follow.*' Here is the story of Helen, and of the judgement of Paris, of the gathering of the heroes, and the siege of Troy; of Achilles, reared by the Centaur on wild honey and the marrow of lions; of Odysseus who volunteered to steal the Palladium, the Luck of Troy; and how he planned and carried out the great strategy of the first Wooden Horse; and of his many adventures on his long, long journey home to Greece.

This is the companion volume to the author's *Tales of the Greek Heroes*. It is impossible to put an age group to such a work. The stories have not lived and been told again and again for over three thousand years without good reason, and they have so much to give to both young and old. This telling is wonderfully easy and inviting and, like the companion volume, excellent for reading aloud. It has new illustrations by Pauline Baynes.

Donation from the library of
Jose Pedro Segundo
1922 - 2022
Please pass freely to others readers so
that everyone can enjoy this book!

THE TALE OF TROY

RETOLD FROM
THE ANCIENT AUTHORS BY

Roger Lancelyn Green

★

'The tale of Troy divine'
MILTON

★

ILLUSTRATED BY

Pauline Baynes

PENGUIN BOOKS

Penguin Books Ltd, Harmondsworth, Middlesex, England
Penguin Books Inc., 7110 Ambassador Road, Baltimore, Maryland 21207, U.S.A.
Penguin Books Australia Ltd, Ringwood, Victoria, Australia

—

First published 1958
Reprinted 1961, 1964, 1965, 1967, 1970, 1971

—

Copyright © Roger Lancelyn Green, 1958

—

Made and printed in Great Britain
by Richard Clay (The Chaucer Press), Ltd,
Bungay, Suffolk
Set in Monotype Baskerville

This book is sold subject to the condition
that it shall not, by way of trade or otherwise,
be lent, re-sold, hired out, or otherwise circulated
without the publisher's prior consent in any form of
binding or cover other than that in which it is
published and without a similar condition
including this condition being imposed
on the subsequent purchaser

TO THE MEMORY OF
TWO FAVOURITE AUTHORS

Rider Haggard and Andrew Lang

WHO TOGETHER WROTE

The World's Desire

WHICH FIRST LED ME TO
THE STUDY OF
GREEK LEGEND AND
LITERATURE

*

Sweet was your song of the world's desire
    When life was yours: now your days are sped
I set at your feet my Lydian lyre,
    And my Phrygian flute to mark your head.

Anonymous Greek Epitaph

CONTENTS

List of Illustrations 8

1. THE MARRIAGE OF PELEUS AND THETIS 9
2. THE JUDGEMENT OF PARIS 23
3. HELEN OF SPARTA 33
4. THE GATHERING OF THE HEROES 47
5. THE SIEGE OF TROY 59
6. THE ADVENTURE OF RHESUS 73
7. THE DEATH OF HECTOR 83
8. NEOPTOLEMUS AND PHILOCTETES 97
9. THE THEFT OF THE LUCK OF TROY 109
10. THE WOODEN HORSE 123
11. THE FALL OF TROY 135
12. AGAMEMNON AND HIS CHILDREN 149
13. THE ADVENTURES OF MENELAUS 161
14. THE WANDERINGS OF ODYSSEUS 175
15. ODYSSEUS IN ITHACA 191
16. THE LAST OF THE HEROES 203

Author's Note 210
The Gods and Goddesses of Ancient Greece 213
Map of the Trojan Wars 214–15

LIST OF ILLUSTRATIONS

And Chiron taught him . . . how to play the lyre   20

Paris   29

Accompanying him as one in a dream, but taking
the baby Nicostratus with her   45

So Iphigenia . . . went steadfastly to her death   57

It smote the round shield of Paris and passed
through it   70

Hector . . . stretched out his arms to Astyanax, but
the child shrank away crying   76

'The ships are on fire and most of the Greek kings
wounded . . .'   86

And each day he trailed the body of Hector round
the walls of Troy   94

Sadly and bitterly he limped away to his cave   106

He snatched the sword from his side and struck
Corythus dead with a single blow   112

'But there stands in the midst of the ruins a great
Wooden Horse the like of which we have never
seen'   125

All that night she sat in her window with a bright
lamp beside her   132

But she clung to the statue of Athena and begged
him to spare her   140

While he struggled in this silken web, she struck him
down with an axe   152

Proteus woke and turned himself into a fierce lion   167

Odysseus instructed his men to bind him to the mast   186

Odysseus set an arrow to the string   198

This wounded Odysseus, who never recovered, but
fell quietly asleep   206

CHAPTER I

THE MARRIAGE OF
PELEUS AND THETIS

*

For late between them rose a bitter strife
    In Peleus' halls upon his wedding day,
When Peleus took him an immortal wife,
    And there was bidden all the gods' array,
    Save Discord only; yet she brought dismay,
And cast an apple on the bridal board.

ANDREW LANG
Helen of Troy

CHAPTER ONE

To the ancient Greeks the Siege of Troy was the greatest and most important event in the Age of the Heroes – that age of wonder when the Immortals who dwelt on Olympus and whom they worshipped as gods, mingled with mankind and took a visible part in their affairs.

The fall of Troy marks the place where legend ends and history begins; yet that great adventure had its beginnings in the early myths of the making of the world: for the Tale of Troy starts with the story of Prometheus.*

Now Prometheus was a Titan, a giant out of the earliest ages of the world who was himself an Immortal, and although he lacked the powers of Zeus, he could do what even Zeus could not: he could foresee the future. Also he had the power of love, which at first Zeus lacked, and this love was given to humankind, to the poor mortals on this earth whom he had helped to fashion.

In the days before man was made, so the old stories said, Zeus fought and overthrew his own terrible father, Cronos – a horrible ogre who swallowed his children in case they should rebel against him. Prometheus helped Zeus in this righteous war, and helped him also to make Mankind to people the devastated earth. But then, out of

* See *Tales of the Greek Heroes* by Roger Lancelyn Green (Puffin Books, 030119 4).

his great love, Prometheus disobeyed Zeus and stole fire from Heaven as a gift to Man which should make him second only to the Immortals.

In his rage Zeus chained Prometheus to the great Caucasus Mountains beyond the Black Sea. But Prometheus then prophesied that Zeus would fall even as Cronos fell, and that only he could save him – for he alone knew what Zeus must do to avoid his doom.

Zeus threatened, bargained and begged, but all in vain. Then, in his fear and fury he sent a terrible eagle to feed day by day on the liver of the poor immortal Titan – the liver that night by night must grow again. But even under this terrible torture Prometheus would not tell his secret.

Time passed, and Zeus began to learn mercy and love through the suffering of the fear which was always before him: for he knew that Prometheus could see the future truly, and that nothing could change what he saw.

As Zeus began to help men on this earth, the Age of the Heroes came, and Zeus married many mortal women, in spite of the jealousy of Hera his Immortal wife.

The last of the mortal children of Zeus was the greatest of all the Heroes, Heracles the strongest man who ever lived. And while Heracles was wandering about the earth performing his Twelve Labours and ridding it of many an evil creature, Zeus sent him to Caucasus to free Prometheus. There were no conditions attached to this act of

mercy, and Prometheus went quietly back to his
work among the men whom he loved.

But Heracles continued with his great deeds,
finishing with the deed for which Zeus had caused
him to be born, which was to fight on the Immortals' side in the great war with the Giants –
which could not be won unless a mortal hero was
there to slay the Giants when the Immortals had
struck them down.

When that war was over, Zeus felt that for a
while at least he was free from care and might
make merry with the Immortals.

'I will have no other mortal sons,' he said, 'for
Heracles, the hero who saved us from the Giants,
must be the last of these. But I have heard tell of a
lovely sea-nymph called Thetis: she shall be my
bride, and maybe we shall have a daughter who
will be the loveliest woman ever seen among men.'

So Zeus visited the caves of ocean, and found
that Thetis was as lovely and as clever as he had
heard. Then he arranged for a great wedding feast,
and bade all the other Immortals make ready for
it. And even jealous Hera was so happy at that
time that she did not try to prevent it, or to bring
any harm to Thetis as she had always tried to do
where the mortal wives of Zeus were concerned.

Then suddenly the good Titan, Prometheus,
came to Zeus and said:

'Great Zeus, though you treated me cruelly in
the beginning I know that what you did was due
to fear. I would not tell you how to avoid the certain danger which threatened you: the danger of

the son who would cast you out as you cast out Cronos, and rule in your place as you ruled in his. No, though you sent your eagle to prey on me, I would not speak. But you know well that the future, hidden even from you, is sometimes clear to me. Did I not warn you of the coming of the Giants, and that you would only defeat them if there was a human Hero strong and brave enough to fight on your side? That man was Heracles, and the battle fell out as I prophesied.'

Zeus bowed his head and answered:

'Titan Prometheus, it is even as you say. In the beginning I had no love for mortal men, and hated you for stealing fire to give to them. As you say, I was cruel and merciless: but I have learnt through suffering, and I no longer hate you, nor wish you ill, even though you know of the danger which threatens me. To prove this, I sent my son the hero Heracles to shoot the eagle and free you from your bonds, leaving only the Ring on your finger in token of your sufferings for mankind. I asked nothing of you in return for your freedom; and indeed I am glad and contented to see you working again upon the earth for the noble race of men.'

'Although I can see much of the future,' said Prometheus, 'I cannot see how the hearts of men and of Immortals may change. Yours has changed, great Zeus – and now I can speak to the merciful Father of gods and men, and tell you of your danger and how to avert it. Listen to the prophecy which I have known from the beginning: "*The son of Thetis shall be greater than his father*." So small a matter, so easy a danger to escape – yet it might have proved the overthrow of great Zeus himself!'

Then Zeus smiled, and uttered a great laugh of joy and relief: and the thunder rumbled, while the summer-lightning flashed out of a clear sky.

'I thank you, Titan Prometheus!' he cried. 'Now once again you are my friend and my helper ... We will marry Thetis to a mortal husband, and their son shall be the last of the Heroes. It is in my mind to cause the great and glorious War of Troy that shall be famous to the end of time. Famous too shall be the names of the Heroes who fight at Troy; but with them the Age of the Heroes shall end, and the Iron Age of ordinary men shall follow.'

The Hero chosen to be the husband of Thetis was Peleus the Argonaut, who had assisted Heracles and Telamon to sack Troy, when King Laomedon refused to keep his word by giving up his magic horses in return for the rescue of Hesione from the sea monster.

It chanced that Peleus killed his friend Eurytion by mistake and in consequence was forced to leave his own country. He went to live at Iolcus where Acastus the son of Pelias was king; and there lived happily for some time.

Now Zeus brought it about that Queen Astydamia fell in love with him, and begged him to run away with her. Peleus refused, he would not do anything so wicked and dishonourable as to steal the wife of his friend. Astydamia was furious, and her love turned to such hatred that she wished only to see Peleus dead. So she went to her husband with a lying tale that Peleus had tried to persuade her to run away with him, and had threatened to carry her off by force if she refused.

Naturally King Acastus was furious: he did not wish to kill Peleus, who was his guest, but he decided to cause his death. So he and his lords took Peleus out hunting on Mount Pelion, and they proposed a contest to see who could kill the most game that day.

Peleus was a skilful hunter, moreover he possessed a magic sword, given to him by the Immortals in reward for his virtue, which made him always successful in the chase and always victorious in battle. On this occasion, as he suspected trickery, whenever he killed an animal, he cut out its tongue which he put away in his pouch.

At the end of the hunt, Acastus and his followers claimed all the spoils as their own, and jeered at Peleus for having killed nothing.

'You have hunted well,' said Peleus quietly, 'but I have hunted better: for I slew just as many animals as I have tongues here in my pouch!' And with that he produced his spoils, and made Acastus and his friends look thoroughly silly.

But it happened a little later in the day that Peleus fell asleep, lying on the lonely mountainside, and Acastus stole his sword and hid it in a pile of dirt. That done, he and his friends went softly away, leaving Peleus alone.

Evening came, and Peleus woke to find himself deserted, unarmed and surrounded by the wild Centaurs, who drew near to kill him. But one of them, Chiron the wise who had trained Jason as a boy, came to his rescue, found the sword and brought him in safety to his own cave.

There he taught Peleus many things, and finally instructed him how he should catch and hold the sea-nymph Thetis, his destined bride.

Peleus did as he was instructed, lying in wait for her on the sea-shore at the foot of Pelion, and catching her unawares. She changed herself in turn into fire, water, wind, a tree, a bird, a tiger, a lion, a serpent and a cuttle-fish: and when she was a fish, Peleus seized her so tightly and held her so fast that she gave up the struggle and returned to her own shape.

Then Peleus led her unwillingly up Pelion to Chiron's cave, but soon she grew happy again and consented to become his wife: for Zeus promised her that she should have a son who would be the most famous Hero to fight at Troy; and that, meanwhile, all the Immortals would attend her wedding.

On the slope of Pelion, by the cave of wise Chiron the good old Centaur, such a wedding-feast was prepared as had never before been seen on earth. The divine food of the Immortals, sweet Nectar and the scented Ambrosia, was brought from Olympus in golden jugs and dishes and set upon silver tables; and all the Immortals gathered to the feast. The Muses sang sweetly to the company, and the Nymphs danced for them, while Hephaestus filled the cave with cunningly wrought flame that harmed nobody, but shed a heavenly radiance over all.

The Immortals gave wondrous gifts to the honoured bridegroom: there was a matchless spear of ash-wood hewn by Chiron, polished by Athena and pointed by Hephaestus; and two deathless horses Balius and Xanthus, the gift of Poseidon.

But one Immortal was forgotten that day, and her name was Eris. She was hated by all the other dwellers on Olympus, for she was disagreeable and mean; her other names were 'Strife' and 'Discord'. But she arrived – suddenly and quite uninvited, at the banquet.

'I have come!' she cried harshly, 'and I bring with me a present!' She cast a Golden Apple on the table, and went laughing away; and on the apple were written these words: 'For the Fairest.'

As she had intended, discord broke out immediately where all had been peace and happiness before, and there was strife as to who could claim the golden apple.

'It is mine!' cried Hera. 'To me the Queen of Olympus, it belongs by right.'

'I claim it,' said Athena, 'I, the eldest daughter of Zeus. And I will prove my right to it . . . Not for nothing am I the Immortal Lady of Wisdom!'

'You are both mistaken,' murmured Aphrodite gently. 'It is mine. No one else has any right to take it. Am not I the Immortal Lady of Beauty and of Love?'

Zeus stilled the wrangling of the three Immortals for the moment, and the wedding ended without its brightness having been marred.

Peleus and his lovely bride thanked their Immortal guests, bade farewell to kindly Chiron and came down from Pelion to dwell in their kingdom by the sea. Before long Peleus ruled Iolcus also, having deposed Acastus and his wicked queen.

The people of his own land were delighted to welcome King Peleus, the most virtuous of men, who had been honoured so greatly by the Immortals:

'Thrice and four-times blessed are you, happy Peleus, son of our old king Aeacus!' they cried. 'And blessed be you also, lovely Queen Thetis, whom Zeus has given you as wife, and honoured your marriage, and given you such wondrous gifts. Truly Zeus has set you apart among men, the Hero more honoured than any other of the heroes!'

The new King and Queen dwelt happily for a while; but as year followed on year Peleus grew troubled. For six sons were born to him and Thetis and all six of them disappeared mysteriously, nor could he learn what became of them. But Thetis grew more and more silent and sad; and her eyes turned with longing to the bright sea-waves under which she had lived before her wedding to Peleus.

Then a seventh son was born, and they called him Achilles.

'See now,' said Thetis, 'I will make our child

invulnerable, so that he may be the greatest of heroes!'

And she carried him away by night to the River Styx, the Black River of the Underworld, and dipped him in the swift-flowing stream. But, fearful lest he should be drowned or washed away, she held him by the heel; and the heel and instep alone remained untouched by the magic water.

When she carried him home, Peleus breathed a sigh of relief that the child was still alive and well. But he determined to watch carefully, and that night he remained awake, though pretending to be asleep.

Presently he saw his wife slip quietly out of bed, take the baby from the cradle, and, having anointed him with Ambrosia, advanced towards the fire. He watched anxiously, and saw Thetis place the child in the heart of the flames.

At that he leapt out of bed with a cry, snatched Achilles from the fire and turned in fury upon Thetis.

But she exclaimed: 'Oh fool, fool! Had you left him, he would have become immortal, and never known old age! For all I had to do was to burn the mortal part of him away, after annointing him with the food of the gods. True, our other sons perished in the flames – but this time I would have been successful, for he had been dipped in Styx and so was invulnerable.'

Then she cried aloud: 'Farewell now, Peleus the foolish. Never more shall you call me wife, for I go back to the sea, never to return to you again.'

Then she fled away like a breath of wind, passed from the palace as swiftly as a dream and leapt into the sea.

Peleus sorrowed deeply at the loss of his lovely

And Chiron taught him . . . how to play the lyre

wife, and he never married again, though he lived to sad old age.

Meanwhile he took the baby Achilles to Mount Pelion and entrusted him to the wise Centaur, Chiron. There the boy dwelt, feeding on the marrow of lions, on wild honey and on the flesh of fawns; and Chiron taught him the arts of riding and hunting, and how to play the lyre.

Thetis, although she had deserted Peleus, still watched over Achilles; and when he was nine, she saw a danger hanging over him and tried to prevent it by hiding him. She dressed him as a girl and sent him to the island of Scyros where Lycomedes was king. There Achilles was hidden among the other maidens who attended on the little princess Deidamia, and indeed he himself almost believed after a time that he was really a girl called Pyrrha.

Thetis did this when the great war between Greece and Troy was about to begin: for she knew that if Achilles went to Troy he would never return.

The beginning of that war went back to the day of her marriage to Peleus. For the golden apple of Discord kept the three Immortals, Hera, Athena and Aphrodite, wrangling and quarrelling until Zeus bade Hermes take them to Mount Ida near Troy and let a shepherd called Paris judge between them.

CHAPTER 2

THE JUDGEMENT OF PARIS

*

Was this the face that launched a thousand ships
And burnt the topless towers of Ilion?
Sweet Helen, make me immortal with a kiss!

MARLOWE
Dr Faustus

CHAPTER TWO

AFTER Heracles, Peleus and Telamon killed King Laomedon and destroyed the old town of Troy, his youngest son Priam became king. He called together the Trojans from near and far, and at his direction they built a new city, larger, stronger, with great gates and walls and towers.

He ruled there in peace and the land grew rich. His Queen, Hecuba, bore him many handsome sons, the eldest of whom was called Hector. But just before the second son, Paris, was born, Queen Hecuba dreamt a terrible dream.

She dreamt that the child was born, but instead of an ordinary baby it turned out to be a Fury (such as those daughters of Hades whom the grim Lord of Death sends out to work vengeance on the wicked), a Fury with a hundred hands and every hand holding a lighted torch. In her dream the Fury rushed through Troy setting all on fire and pushing down the newly-built towers.

When she awoke, Hecuba told Priam of her dream, and he sent for all the wise men of Troy to see if any of them could say what it meant. They told him that, if he lived, Paris would bring about the ruin of his country and the destruction of Troy itself; and they advised Priam to kill the child quickly.

Priam was very sad at this, yet when the baby boy was born he gave him to a faithful servant and bade him carry the child far away on to the lonely slopes of Mount Ida, and leave him there to be eaten by wild beasts. The servant did as he was told, leaving the child near the den of a fierce bear. Five days later, when hunting on Ida, the man revisited the place and to his amazement found the baby Paris alive and well in the bear's very lair, lying among the cubs.

'The child must be fated to live,' thought the servant, 'if even the wild beasts feed and tend it,' and he picked up Paris and took him to his own cottage. Here he brought up the boy as his son, teaching him to hunt, and to tend the flocks and herds on the mountain slopes.

Paris grew up strong and brave, and from the beginning he was one of the handsomest boys to be seen, so fine indeed that the nymph Oenone fell in love with him, and they were married and lived in a beautiful cave on Mount Ida; and there a son was born to them called Corythus.

Paris took great interest in the herd of cattle which was his charge, and when he was still quite a boy he drove away a band of robbers who tried to steal them. He was particularly proud of the herd bull, a beautiful milk-white animal stronger and finer than any other bull on Ida. He was so confident in the superior merits of his bull that he offered to crown with gold any finer than his own.

One day, as a jest, the Immortal Ares turned himself into a bull and got Hermes to drive him up Ida to compete with Paris's animal. The stranger was even more beautiful and stronger than the champion, and Paris without hesitation awarded it the promised crown.

It was on account of this scrupulous fairness that Zeus, who refused to judge them himself, sent the three lovely Immortals, Hera, Athena and Aphrodite, to have their contest for the ownership of the golden apple of Discord decided by Paris.

Hermes, the Immortal Guide, led the way to Mount Ida, and there found Paris, young, strong and handsome in his goatskin cloak, seated on the hillside playing sweet tunes on his pipe, with his herdsman's crook laid beside him.

Looking up, Paris beheld the Immortal drawing near to him, and knew him by the winged sandals and the herald's wand. Then he would have leapt up and hidden in the woods, but Hermes called to him:

'Do not fear, herdsman Paris – you who are greater than you yet know. I come to you from Zeus, who knows of your fairness in judgement, and I bring with me three Immortal Queens. You must choose which of them is the fairest – for such is the will of Zeus.'

Then Paris answered: 'Lord Hermes, I am but a mortal, how can I judge of Immortal loveliness? And if judge I do, how can I escape the vengeance of those who are not chosen?'

'They will abide by your decision,' answered Hermes, 'and it is a mortal choice that Zeus requires. As for what will come of it, that Zeus alone knows, for all this happens by his will.'

Then the three Immortals drew near, and Paris

stood for a little, dazzled by their shining loveliness.

Presently Hera came to him, tall and stately, a Queen of Queens with a shimmering diadem on her beautiful forehead and her large eyes shining with majesty:

'Choose me,' she said in her rich voice, 'and I will make you lord of all Asia. You shall have power greater than any king: if you will it, Greece shall be yours also . . .'

Paris looked upon her, and the beauty he saw was the beauty of power, of sway and dominion; he saw all his dreams of such ambition given shape and form in this lovely Immortal Queen.

He gasped and hid his eyes; and when he looked again Athena stood before him in quiet dignity. From her eyes shone wisdom and thought, and the helmet shimmered on her head, in token of deeds done and not merely planned.

'I will give you wisdom,' she said, 'you shall be the wisest of men, and the kings of the earth shall come to you for counsel. With this wisdom you may conquer in war and rule if so you choose.'

Then Paris forgot his dreams of kingship and majesty: instead he saw knowledge and skill in all arts and in all learning – and they took the form of the wise-eyed, dignified Immortal whose cool hand rested for a moment on his shoulder.

Paris bowed his head, and when he raised it again he saw Aphrodite, lovelier than a dream of beauty, standing before him. Her garments were spun by the Graces and dyed in the flowers of spring – in crocus and hyacinth, in flourishing violet and the rose's lovely bloom, so sweet and delicious, and in those heavenly buds the flowers of the narcissus and lily. Her face and form were beautiful beyond imagining, and her voice was soft and thrilling:

'Take me,' she murmured, 'and forget harsh wars and cares of state. Take my beauty and leave the sceptre and the torch of wisdom. I know nothing of battles or of learning: what has Aphrodite to do with the sword or the pen? In place of wisdom, in place of sovereignty, I will give you the most beautiful woman upon earth to be your bride. Helen of Sparta is her name, and she shall be called the World's Desire and beauty's very self.'

Paris did not hesitate, but gave the Golden Apple to Aphrodite, and she laughed sweetly and triumphantly.

'Now Paris,' she said, 'I will be ever at your side and I will lead you to the golden Helen!'

But Hera and Athena turned away with anger in their eyes, and from that moment began their hatred of Troy and of all the Trojans.

Paris slept on the flowery slope of Mount Ida, and when he awoke he could not tell whether he had given judgement in a dream or in reality. But now he could no longer be happy with Oenone, nor as a herdsman in the woods and on the mountain slopes. For, waking and asleep, he saw the fair form of Aphrodite and heard her voice; and sometimes the form and the voice changed and took the

Paris

shape and tones of a mortal woman, more lovely than any dream, who was destined to be his bride. He waited to see what Aphrodite would do to fulfil her promise, and it was not long before things began to happen.

King Priam, believing his son Paris to be dead, held funeral games each year in memory of him, and this year he sent his servants up on to Ida for a bull to be the chief prize.

They chose the magnificent white bull which was Paris's pride, and drove it away, in spite of all he could say to persuade them to leave it. So, half in anger and half in curiosity, Paris followed them down to Troy, and found a great crowd gathered to watch the chariot race.

When this was ended, Priam declared that the boxing match would be open to all comers – and Paris at once entered for it. He boxed so well that he won the laurel crown; and, competing in the foot-race, won that also. The other sons of Priam were furious that a strange herdsman should win, and they challenged him themselves; but he out-ran them all, and having won three events was declared victor of the day and winner of the prize bull.

Then Hector and his brother Deiphobus were so angry that they drew their swords to slay Paris. But the old servant flung himself at Priam's feet crying:

'My lord king, this is Paris, the son whom you bade me cast out to die on the mountain-side!'

Then Paris was welcomed eagerly by the King and Queen, and by his brothers as well, and was soon reinstated as a prince of Troy.

But his sister Cassandra, who was a prophetess, cried aloud that if Paris were allowed to live, Troy was doomed. Priam, however, merely smiled at her, and answered playfully:

'Better that Troy should fall than that I should lose this wonderful new son of mine!'

Now Cassandra suffered this fate: that she should speak the truth and not be believed. For she had offended Apollo and, since he could not take from her the gift of prophecy which he had bestowed, he took this means of rendering the gift useless.

After a while, Aphrodite instructed Paris to build ships and sail to Greece, and she sent her son Aeneas with him. For Zeus had been angered with Aphrodite when she boasted that she had made all the Immortals fall in love with mortals, except the Three Heavenly Maidens, Hestia, Athena and Artemis, and he had made Aphrodite herself wed a human. She chose Anchises, a prince of Troy, the grandson of King Ilus and cousin of Priam, who was at the time a herdsman on Mount Ida. There Aeneas was born, and Aphrodite warned Anchises that he would be punished if ever he boasted of his Immortal bride: but boast he did, one day when he had feasted over-merrily, and on the instant a flash of fire struck him to the ground. Yet, for the sake of Aeneas, and also for his own virtues, Aphrodite spared his life: but he went lame from that day.

When the ships were built, Paris sailed joyously forth over the dancing waves, though Cassandra prophesied of ills to come, and Oenone wept, lonely and deserted, in her mountain cave.

CHAPTER 3

HELEN OF SPARTA

*

Even such (for sailing hither I saw far hence,
And where Eurotas hollows his moist rock
Nigh Sparta with a strenuous-hearted stream)
Even such I saw their sisters; one swan-white,
The little Helen, and less fair than she
Fair Clytemnestra, grave as pasturing fawns
Who feed and fear some arrow . . .

A. C. SWINBURNE
Atalanta in Calydon

CHAPTER THREE

THE bride whom Paris went forth to seek at the command of Aphrodite, and to carry away to Troy, had already been sought in marriage by all the Heroes of Greece. She had even been carried away once when she was a young girl – by Theseus, the famous king of Athens who, in his old age, was far from being the noble Hero of his earlier years.

Theseus had always been violent and impulsive, but it was only after he made friends with Pirithous, King of the Lapiths, that he turned from good to evil.

This friendship began when the wild women called Amazons landed in Greece and marched to attack Athens. Theseus defeated them on the Hill of Ares, or Areopagus, and drove them away. But Pirithous, thinking that Theseus would be wearied and weakened after so fierce a battle, chose this moment to march towards Athens with his lawless followers.

But Theseus marched to meet him, and there would have been a fierce battle if the two kings had not decided suddenly to make peace instead. For when they met, each loved the other at sight, and swore a firm friendship.

Theseus then visited the land of the Lapiths to attend the wedding of Pirithous, and at the feast a strange battle broke out. Among the guests were many Centaurs, and these wild half-men grew drunk with wine and carried off the bride and all the other women present.

A great battle developed in which the Centaurs were driven far away; and after that, King Pirithous was even more devoted to Theseus than ever – though he lost his bride in the battle.

Now Theseus was one of the great heroes of Greece, second only to Heracles himself, and his deeds had won him great fame. He had cleared the land of many pests and monsters, had slain the Minotaur and saved Athens from its tribute to King Minos, besides sailing to Colchis with Jason and the Argonauts, helping to hunt the Calydonian Boar, and defeating the fierce invasion of Amazons.

But after his friendship with Pirithous began, he seemed to lose his heroic virtues. He became cruel and despotic, was banished for a year from Athens for a murder, and while away caused the death of his own son Hippolytus in a moment of rage and jealousy.

In the past he had done much for Athens, and he stood as an example of a just and pious king; but now the Athenians began to murmur against him and to wish that his cousin Menestheus, who was in fact the rightful heir, sat on the throne in his place.

Theseus was middle-aged by now, but he and Pirithous decided suddenly that they must both marry again:

'But *we* cannot stoop to ordinary maidens!' cried Pirithous. '*Our* wives must be daughters of Zeus, no less!'

Theseus agreed to anything Pirithous suggested, and even swore the most solemn oath possible that he would help him to capture and carry away who ever his chosen bride might be. And Pirithous vowed to do the same for Theseus.

Then they cast about for daughters of Zeus. Now this was difficult, for Alcmena had been Zeus's last mortal wife, and Heracles his last human child. But about this time it began to be rumoured that King Tyndareus of Sparta had a daughter who was likely to grow into the most beautiful woman in the world. It was also said that Zeus, having been father of the strongest man who ever lived, was determined, for purposes of his own, to have a daughter who would be the most beautiful woman of all; and further, it was added that he had visited Queen Leda in the form of a swan, and that their daughter Helen had been hatched out of an egg.

However this might be, Helen of Sparta, even at the age of twelve, was 'beauty's very self', far outshining even her sister Clytemnestra. Theseus heard of her, and decided that here was his destined bride.

So he and Pirithous set out for Sparta, seized Helen while she was worshipping in the Temple of Artemis and carried her off to Athens. But the Athenians were so disgusted at what Theseus had done that he took her to the castle of Aphidna not far away, and left her there attended by his mother Aethra, and guarded by a band of faithful followers.

It was now the turn of Pirithous to choose a wife: for according to their agreement, neither was to marry until both their brides had been captured. Now Pirithous, in his mad pride and irreverence, declared that only Persephone herself, the daughter of Zeus and Dementer and wife of Hades, would satisfy him. Theseus tried to persuade him to aim a little lower, but in vain.

So the two ravishers set off for the Realm of the Dead, and Theseus, profiting by all that he had heard from Heracles concerning his journey to and from that dread land when performing the last of his Labours for King Eurystheus, led the way to the Cave of Taenarum.

Down by the steep, dangerous paths they went, and came in time to the gloomy kingdom where Hades reigned. That Lord of many Guests knew quite well on what impious errand they came, but he hid his knowledge and made them welcome.

'None of the sons of men have ever visited me here while still alive,' he said grimly. For Orpheus was the son of Apollo, while Dionysus and Heracles both had Zeus for their father. 'And, being still mortal, only those three have ever returned living to the world above . . . Therefore, daring humans, come now and feast with me!'

But Theseus, knowing that those who eat of the food of the Dead can never return to the land of the Living, refused the invitation politely, appealing to Persephone who had eaten six seeds of the pomegranate when Hades carried her off, and so could only return to earth for six months of the year.

'Then at least come and sit with me,' said Hades, and he led them to a royal throne by the side of the softly moving Lethe, the River of Forgetfulness. All unsuspecting, Theseus and Pirithous seated themselves on the carven stone – and at once it held them and they became part of it, so that there was no way of rising without tearing away their own flesh.

Then Hades laughed grimly: 'Here is my Queen, Persephone, daughter of Zeus!' he said. 'Come, take her if you can, you rash and impious men!' But they could not move, though weaving coils of serpents hissed about them, and the Furies, servants of Hades, tormented them; nor did Cerberus, the triple Hound of Hell, fail to fasten his teeth in them from time to time.

It is said that some years later Heracles, while on a visit to Hades and Persephone, begged for the release of his friend and managed to tear him from his terrible seat. But after his return Theseus did not become King of Athens again; and he soon perished miserably in exile. Certainly Pirithous never again saw the light of day, and Hades moved his terrible seat near to the wheel on which his father Ixion suffered.

Meanwhile Helen was still a prisoner at Aphidna; so her brothers Castor and Polydeuces collected an army and set out to rescue her. They laid siege to Aphidna, captured it and razed it to the ground, after they had recovered Helen and taken Aethra, the mother of Theseus, to be her slave.

Then they marched to Athens to punish Theseus himself; but not finding him, and being welcomed as deliverers by the citizens, they made peace and set Menestheus, the rightful king, on the throne.

Helen, safe again in Sparta, grew up into the loveliest girl ever seen, as Zeus had intended, and King Tyndareus became anxious about her. For just as Theseus had carried her off, so he feared that some other king or prince of Greece might steal her also. He became even more anxious when his brave sons Castor and Polydeuces were no longer there to protect her.

For on a time a bitter quarrel broke out between them and their cousins Idas and Lynceus, the sons of Aphareus brother of King Tyndareus, who reigned at Messene near Sparta. His third brother, Leucippus, had promised his daughters in marriage to Castor and Polydeuces, but Lynceus and Idas obtained possession of them, either by bribery or by force, and carried them off into Arcadia.

Castor and Polydeuces therefore set out with a band of followers to punish their cousins and retrieve their brides. When the two armies met, a truce was called, and Lynceus said:

'Let us not shed blood unnecessarily. We both want these same girls, cannot we decide the question by single combat? I will fight with Castor, and who ever slays the other shall lead away both maidens without let or hindrance:'

The Spartan twins agreed to this, and all men gathered round to watch the battle as Castor and Lynceus made ready for their deadly combat. With the crests nodding above their helmets they approached one another, their great shields held ready and their spear-points quivering.

Then they tilted at each other, trying vainly to get past the protective shields, but their spears stuck at last in the tough bronze and leather, and snapped off the points. Then they flung away the useless shafts, snatched out their glittering swords, and lashed at one another.

Many a time did Castor smite on his enemy's broad shield and horse-hair crest; and many a time keen-eyed Lynceus smote back, and once even shore away the scarlet plume. Then, as he aimed the sharp sword at the left knee, Castor drew back his left foot, and hacked off the fingers from the hand of Lynceus. At this Lynceus cast away his sword and fled towards the tomb of his father Aphareus behind which Idas had concealed himself.

But as he reached it, Castor's sword pierced his body and he fell dead to the ground.

Joyfully Castor turned to claim the victory and clasp his bride. But as he did so, Idas rose up from behind the tomb, where he had been hiding, and tore away a great stone from it, which he dashed down upon Castor's head.

Brave Castor fell dying to the ground; but Idas did not live long to rejoice in his treachery, for

Zeus hurled down a thunderbolt from Olympus, and blotted him from the face of the earth.

In desperate sorrow Polydeuces bent over his dying brother; and when he saw that there was no hope for him, he prayed:

'Father Zeus, Immortal son of Cronos, when, oh when will there come a release from this sorrow? Let me die also, king of life and death; let me not survive my beloved brother!'

Zeus, deeply moved, spoke out of the thunder cloud in which he had drawn nigh:

'My son, I had thought to make you immortal, to be a guide to men at sea in times of trouble. Do you now prefer death, and the dim land of Hades where your brother must dwell, rather than immortality, with a seat at the heavenly banquet on Olympus? There you were to sit between Athena and Ares, while dainty Hebe served you with the food and wine of the Immortals.'

But Polydeuces answered: 'If Castor cannot share it with me, then I would rather renounce the banquet of the Immortals, and wander in the shadowy realm where Hades is king.'

Then said Zeus: 'For this great love of yours, I decree that both of you shall sit on Olympus and go forth to do my bidding on the deep. But Hades cannot be deprived of his due, so day and day about, you must be as the dead in the world of shadows; and day and day about you may tread the sky with us the Immortals.'

So it came about that neither Castor nor Polydeuces dwelt any longer among men, but became the 'Dioscuri', the 'Striplings of Zeus', and had their Twin Stars in heaven, and brought kindly succour and guidance to those in peril on the sea.

King Tyndareus mourned the death of his two brave sons, and was troubled more and more as to what should chance on account of his beautiful daughter, Helen.

Then at last he sent heralds throughout Greece and the Islands, proclaiming that the time had come when he would choose her a husband; and that her husband should also rule over Sparta and defend it against all invaders.

The kings and princes of Hellas, the sons of those who had fared with Jason in Quest of the Golden Fleece, and of those who had stood beside Meleager when the Boar of Calydon was slain, came hastening to Sparta.

There came Odysseus the wise son of Laertes, King of Ithaca: and Diomedes son of Tydeus; Menestheus of Athens came, and Aias the son of Oileus. From rich Mycenae and Tiryns came Agamemnon and Menelaus, whose father was a cousin of Eurystheus and had succeeded to his throne; Eumelus was there also, the son of Admetus and Alcestis, and Philoctetes who now owned the bow and arrows of Heracles. There was Ajax the son of Telamon, the old friend of Heracles who had helped him to sack Troy; and there was Ajax's half-brother, young Teucer, whose mother was that Hesione whom Heracles had saved from the sea-monster, and many others whose names were soon to become famous.

Seeing the numbers of them, Tyndareus grew afraid lest if he chose one, some of the others might try to steal the bride and start a disastrous war. Not knowing what to do, he consulted Odysseus the Prince of Ithaca, who, though only a young man, was already famous for his wisdom and cunning.

'Why,' said Odysseus, 'the obvious thing is to make all the suitors swear a most solemn oath before you announce your choice. Make them swear to abide by your choice; to defend whoever you choose and come to his aid with a good array of men and ships if anyone, whoever he may be, should steal Helen or carry her off.'

Tyndareus thought this an excellent scheme, and the suitors all agreed to it, swearing, most solemnly, an oath that none of them would dare to break.

Tyndareus chose Menelaus as the husband of Helen; the young, brave prince of Mycenae, whose elder brother, Agamemnon, would soon be king. To make still more certain alliance with Mycenae, Tyndareus gave his other daughter Clytemnestra to be Agamemnon's wife. And in gratitude to Odysseus he persuaded his brother Icarius to give him his daughter, Penelope, in marriage.

When all these things were settled, and Helen was married to Menelaus, the kings and princes departed to their own homes, and peace descended upon the lovely land of Lacedaemon of which Sparta was the chief city. And very soon Tyndareus gave up the throne and retired to enjoy his old age in peace and quiet, and Menelaus and Helen became King and Queen. They had a lovely daughter called Hermione and a son Nicostratus, and lived in great happiness for some years in beautiful Lacedaemon – until Paris the Trojan came.

To begin with, all seemed fair and honest. Paris told them that he was visiting Greece on an embassy from King Priam, to inquire after his aunt, Hesione, who was now the wife of King Telamon of Salamis. So Menelaus greeted his guest kindly, and he and Helen entertained the Trojan strangers for nine days.

On the tenth a message came for Menelaus that his mother's father Catreus had died in Crete, and he was wanted at the funeral. Suspecting no evil, he sailed away, leaving Helen to entertain the guests until they were ready to leave for Salamis.

Next day Paris said farewell to Helen and embarked with Aeneas and all his followers. But that night he returned to Sparta, and next morning he was on the high seas with Helen aboard his ship.

For once Paris had seen the beauty of Helen, he cared for nothing in the world but to win her – by fair means or foul. And Aphrodite, having promised, was ready to help him with her magic arts.

Some say that he carried off Helen by main force, and robbed the palace of all its treasures at the same time; others, that by the spells of Aphrodite Paris was able to assume the form of Menelaus, and that Helen went with him readily, leaving her beloved daughter Hermione without a thought, and accompanying him as one in a dream, but taking the baby Nicostratus with her.

Away they sailed, and Hera called up a storm-wind to blow them out of their course. But they landed on Aphrodite's island of Cyprus; and after-

Accompanying him as one in a dream, but taking the baby Nicostratus with her

wards visited Sidon (where Paris treacherously slew the king and stole his treasure), and so back to Troy by way of Phoenicia and Egypt.

And when Paris reached Troy at last, bringing the beautiful Helen with him, their wedding took place amid the rejoicing of the Trojans. For when Cassandra stood on the citadel, tearing her hair and crying: 'Woe, woe to Troy! Helen has come, who will bring ruin and death to us all,' Priam replied that death and ruin were worth risking merely to look upon the beauty of Helen and to have her at Troy. All the Trojans agreed with him, and vowed never to give her up.

But she dwelt among them in sadness and shame, once the magic of Aphrodite had faded. And from that day forth Helen wore on her breast the shining Star-stone which she found waiting for her in the citadel of Troy. Moment by moment the red drops from the ruby heart of the Star fell on her snowy raiment, fell and vanished – fell and vanished – and left no stain: even as if the drops were the drops of blood shed for her, the innocent cause of so much war and sorrow.

CHAPTER 4

THE GATHERING OF THE HEROES

*

In Troy, there lies the scene. From isles of Greece
The princes orgulous . . . their vow is made
To ransack Troy; within whose strong immures
The ravisht Helen, Menelaus' queen,
With wanton Paris sleeps; and that's the quarrel.

SHAKESPEARE
Troilus and Cressida

CHAPTER FOUR

No sooner had Paris the Trojan sailed away carrying Helen with him, than Hera, Queen of the Immortals and his sworn enemy, sent her messenger Iris to tell Menelaus of his loss. Iris was the bright sister of the evil Harpies, and the sworn servant of the Immortals, and of Hera in particular; and when she went on a message, Zeus spread his rainbow as a bridge for her from heaven to earth.

Full of sorrow at the loss of Helen, and anger against the daring Trojan thief, Menelaus hastened back to Greece. First of all he went to his brother Agamemnon, lord of rich Mycenae, who was the husband of Helen's sister, Clytemnestra.

'The beautiful Helen has been stolen away by Trojan Paris!' he cried. 'Now is the time to gather all the kings and princes of Greece, according to their oath when all were her suitors at Sparta, and set sail for Troy to exact vengeance!'

Agamemnon was not quite as eager to go to war as his brother was, and first of all sent a swift ship to Troy, demanding Helen's instant return. But the ship, making the crossing in three days, reached Troy long before Paris, and Priam sent back an insolent answer:

'How can you Greeks make so much fuss about one missing woman? First of all return the women of Asia whom you have stolen – Medea of Colchis, and my own sister Hesione!'

This reply angered Agamemnon: for Medea had come to Greece of her own wish, and brought much evil to Jason by so doing. As for Hesione, Laomedon had promised her to Heracles if he could save her from the sea-monster. But the theft of Helen was a crime committed by a guest against his host – one of the worst of sins in Greek eyes.

So Agamemnon sent out heralds through all Greece bidding the kings and princes gather men and ships, and meet at the port of Aulis, on the coast not very far from Thebes.

Presently the heralds began to return, bringing news of the eagerness with which the heroes were answering the summons. But one startling piece of news brought back by them was that Odysseus of Ithaca, son of Laertes the Argonaut, the very man who had suggested the oath which bound the suitors of Helen, could not come – for he had gone mad.

Anxious to investigate this extraordinary rumour, Agamemnon and Menelaus set out for Ithaca, accompanied by Palamedes the young prince of Nauplia. Sure enough, when they landed it was to find Odysseus ploughing the sand on the sea-shore, with an ox and a horse harnessed to his plough, and sowing salt instead of seed.

He seemed to be very mad indeed: but Palamedes had a suspicious mind, and thought he would test this madness. So he seized Telemachus, the infant son of Odysseus and Penelope and placed him in front of the plough. Sure enough, when

Odysseus saw his beloved son in such danger, he reined in his strange team and made haste to pick up the baby.

After that, his pretence of madness was at an end, and he explained that he had only done so because of an oracle which warned him that if he went to Troy he would not return home for twenty years.

Odysseus loved his island home, and adored his wife and child, so he could never forgive Palamedes for having ruined his clever scheme for avoiding the summons to Troy. Nevertheless he went now with a smile and a shrug, and not one of the heroes did better service in the war than he.

On their voyage to Aulis, Odysseus and Palamedes went out of their way to visit Cyprus, to persuade King Cinyras to join the Greek Allies against Troy. In the end Cinyras promised solemnly to send fifty ships, and Menelaus sailed on to Aulis with the good news. But when the contingent from Cyprus arrived, it consisted of one ship only – which carried forty-nine others, modelled in clay. It was believed by many of the Greeks that Cinyras had in fact bribed Palamedes to relieve him from his promise.

Odysseus also visited Delos, accompanied this time by Menelaus, to beg the aid of the three daughters of King Anius, the son of Apollo. These three wonderful maidens were called 'The Winegrowers', for Dionysus, whose daughter Rhoio was their mother, had given them the magic touch. One of the maidens could turn what she would into wine: the second could produce corn in the same fashion, and the third olives.

King Anius, who had a gift of prophecy from his father, would not at first allow his daughters to go:

'But,' said he, 'why not come and live here – all of you – for nine years? Then I'll see what I can do; for it has been revealed to me that Troy will not fall until the tenth year! And my daughters can feed you here just as well as at Troy!'

Menelaus would not believe this: however he returned with the message. But Agamemnon was already beginning to feel the corrupting joys of absolute power, and he sent Palamedes to fetch the Wine-growers by force – and the maidens fed the Greek army for nine years. In the end they escaped, but were pursued by Agamemnon's orders, and when they were overtaken, prayed to Dionysus for aid, and he turned them into doves – which were ever afterwards held sacred on the lovely little island of Delos.

It was some time before the kings and princes of Greece were all assembled at Aulis with their fleets and armies; but in the end there were one thousand and thirteen ships, with forty-three leaders. And when they were all assembled, there was no wind to waft them across the sea.

Then Calchas, a priest of Apollo, began to prophesy. He was a Trojan traitor who had come to Agamemnon saying that he had left Troy because his foresight told him that Troy must fall: moreover, he said, he could not remain in a city guilty of such a crime as the theft of Helen.

Agamemnon believed everything that Calchas told, for he was very superstitious, and Calchas began by prophesying that Troy would never fall unless Achilles, the young son of the hero Peleus who was too old to come in person, led his people, the Myrmidons, to the war. It was rumoured that young Achilles, aged fifteen by this time, was concealed at the court of King Lycomedes on the island of Scyros, and Odysseus set out at once to find him, accompanied by Diomedes.

On the way Odysseus laid his plans, and Diomedes made ready to play his part. They arrived at Scyros dressed as merchants, though Odysseus drew King Lycomedes aside and gave him a message from Agamemnon demanding that Achilles should be given up to them.

'He is not here,' answered Lycomedes boldly. 'You may look anywhere you like in my palace.'

As search proved of no avail, Odysseus put his scheme into action. Still disguised as a merchant, he visited Princess Deidamia and her maidens carrying a goodly roll of merchandise, which he spread out before them.

'Now then, fair ladies!' he cried. 'Come and take your choice! There are gifts for all of you – a poor return for all King Lycomedes's kindness to us merchants.'

The maidens gathered round, and began fingering and trying on the brooches and jewelled belts, snoods and other trifles. But the maiden Pyrrha lighted upon a sword which was somehow mixed up with all the feminine gewgaws and trumperies, and fingered it longingly. Suddenly a martial trumpet sounded just outside the door, and there was a cry from Diomedes and a clash of weapons. The maidens screamed, and turned to fly, but Pyrrha snatched up the sword, flung off cloak and robe and stood forth to do battle – Achilles revealed in all his young strength and daring.

'Ah-ha!' cried Odysseus. 'Up, son of mighty Peleus and come with us to Troy. No more can guileful Thetis conceal you here; come, and show your metal, and bring honour to your father who in olden days stood beside Heracles, the greatest of heroes!'

So Achilles made haste to collect his troops, and left behind him Princess Deidamia whom he had married in secret, and their young son Neoptolemus. Soon he and his Myrmidons arrived at Aulis; and with him came his cousin Patroclus, some years older than he was, but already his dearest friend.

Now everything seemed ready for the expedition to set out, and Calchas offered up a great sacrifice to the Immortals. While all the chiefs were gathered together round the altar, a blue snake with red markings darted suddenly from beneath the stone, climbed to the top-most branch of a plane-tree which stood close by and there devoured eight baby sparrows in their nest, finishing off by eating the mother-sparrow also. Having done this, the snake was turned immediately into stone.

'An omen!' cried Calchas. 'An omen from Zeus!

He has shown us this sign, late come, of late fulfilment, the fame of which shall never perish. For even as the snake swallowed the eight baby sparrows and then the parent bird, so shall we war against Troy for nine years: but in the tenth year we shall take that wide-wayed city.'

Then the great fleet set sail, with Agamemnon in command of the whole army, and Odysseus, Diomedes and Palamedes as seconds in command, while Achilles was admiral of the fleet. Nestor, the old hero of Pylos, was Agamemnon's chief adviser; and he took heed of his words even more readily than those of the wise Odysseus.

Achilles did not prove a very satisfactory Admiral, for he led the fleet so badly that they landed in Mysia, several hundred miles south of Troy. Then, thinking that they had reached their journey's end, they set to work to ravage the country and burn down the villages, at which Telephus, King of Mysia, who was a son of Heracles, gathered his army together and chased the Greeks back to their ships. Unfortunately for himself, he tripped over a vine and was wounded in the thigh by Achilles.

The Greeks, realizing their mistake, set sail again: but a fearful storm broke upon them, and drove them back towards Greece, scattering the fleet far and wide.

When at length he came to land, Agamemnon found that he and a large portion of the fleet had been driven to his own homeland of Argolis; so he returned to Mycenae while his ships were repaired, and sent messengers bidding the other heroes assemble once more at Aulis the following spring.

Meanwhile King Telephus was suffering so sorely from his wound, which showed no sign of healing, that he consulted an oracle, and was told 'Only the wounder can heal!' Accordingly he set out for Greece, disguised as a beggar, and came to Mycenae where many of the leaders were assembled. Clytemnestra hospitably offered him a place by the fireside, and there he suddenly seized Orestes, the baby son of the King and Queen of Mycenae, from his cradle, and cried:

'I am Telephus, King of Mysia, whom you wronged! If you will cure me of my wound, and swear that no harm shall befall me, I will guide your fleet to Troy. But if you attempt to kill me, I will slay this young prince.'

Then Agamemnon swore the required oath, and Achilles cured Telephus of his wound with the aid of the magic spear which had inflicted it.

Now, with a trustworthy pilot assured, the Greeks assembled once more at Aulis and made ready for the invasion of Troy. But a dead calm lay over all the sea for day after day, and sail they could not. At last the prophet Calchas arose and said:

'King Agamemnon, the Immortal Artemis has caused this calm, to punish you for boasting that you were a better shot than she is. And you will never sail to Troy until you sacrifice to her your daughter Iphigenia.'

Agamemnon was filled with grief, and at first

wished to abandon the whole expedition. But presently he changed his mind and sent Odysseus to fetch Iphigenia.

'Tell my wife, Queen Clytemnestra,' he said, 'that Iphigenia is to come here as a bride. Say that Achilles wishes to marry her, and will not set sail for Troy until after the wedding.'

Believing this, Clytemnestra set out herself with her daughter and arrived at the Greek camp. Here she met Achilles, and greeted him as her future son-in-law: but he was amazed, for not only had he heard nothing of the matter, but was already married to Deidamia.

Very soon Clytemnestra discovered Agamemnon's shameful trick and failing to turn him from his purpose, she begged Achilles to save Iphigenia. Full of indignation against Agamemnon, Achilles agreed to do so; but what was his consternation when he discovered that Calchas had spread abroad his prophecy, and all the army, including the Myrmidons themselves, were clamouring for the sacrifice to be carried out.

To the reproaches of Clytemnestra and the terrified prayers of Iphigenia, Agamemnon answered sadly and bitterly:

'I am no madman, nor have I ceased to love my children. This is a fearful thing, yet I must do it. Unless this sacrifice is made, so Calchas assures me, we can never reach Troy: and all the Greeks are burning to smite the foe. If Paris goes unpunished for the theft of Helen, they believe that the Trojans will come to Greece and steal more women

– steal their wives – steal you and our daughters.
I do not bow to the will of Menelaus: it is not
merely to bring back Helen that we go. But I do
bow to the will of all Greece, and bow I must
whether I will it or not – for Greece is greater far

So Iphigenia . . . went steadfastly to her death

than any personal sorrow. We live for her, to guard
her freedom.'

Clytemnestra would still have struggled against
it, and Achilles offered to fight single-handed, but
Iphigenia rose to the sacrifice:

'I have chosen death,' she said, 'I choose

honour. With me rests the freedom of our beloved land, the honour of our women through many years to come. My death will save them – and my name will be blessed as the name of one who freed Greece from fear and slavery.'

So Iphigenia, hailed by the army as the true conqueror of Troy, went steadfastly to her death. But Immortal Artemis took pity on her youth and on her great courage. As the knife was actually falling and the fire was already kindled, she snatched her away and set a doe in her place.

After that the wind rose strongly from the west, and that great armada set out joyfully in the direction of Troy.

CHAPTER 5

THE SIEGE OF TROY

*

Paint with threads of gold and scarlet, paint the battles
    fought for me,
All the wars for Argive Helen; storm and sack by land
    and sea;
All the tales of loves and sorrows that have been and are
    to be.

Paint the storms of ships and chariots, rain of arrows
    flying far,
Paint the waves of warfare leaping up at beauty like a
    star,
Like a star that pale and trembling hangs above the waves
    of war.

ANDREW LANG
The World's Desire

CHAPTER FIVE

THE Greek fleet did not come to Troy without adventures on the way, even this time when the winds were favourable and the sea was calm. Before landing at Troy they put in to the little island of Tenedos a few miles from the coast, to wait while ambassadors were sent to King Priam, and as they came ashore there they had a brush with the inhabitants, and Achilles killed their chief, Tenes, who was the son of Apollo. Achilles knew then that he must expect the anger of that Immortal Archer, for Thetis had warned him what might happen: but the only person to suffer at the time was Philoctetes, the man who had lit the funeral pyre of Heracles on Mount Oeta, and who still carried the bow and deadly arrows, dipped in the blood of the Hydra, which the dying Hero had given to him. Philoctetes was bitten in the ankle by a snake which crept out from under the altar when the kings were sacrificing to Apollo; and the sore did not heal, and grew so noisome that the other men could not endure the stench of it, nor the cries of the wretched sufferer. So Agamemnon ordered Odysseus to take Philoctetes to the desert island of Lemnos and maroon him there. And there Philoctetes remained nearly ten years, living on the birds and beasts which he managed to shoot with his bow and arrows.

Menelaus and Odysseus then landed near Troy

itself as ambassadors, and marched inland to the city which stood several miles from the shore.

The Trojans received them coldly, but Prince Antenor, cousin of King Priam, made them welcome in his house. Next day, in the assembly of all the Trojan lords and princes, Menelaus and Odysseus asked for Helen to be restored, suitable fines to be paid and hostages given; and they said that if this were done, the Greeks would sail away in peace.

The Trojans admired the broad shoulders and kingly aspect of Menelaus, and still more the wonderful voice and the persuasive words of Odysseus, though he was below medium height and made no flourishes with his hands when he spoke. But Antimachus, who had been bribed by Paris, urged the Trojans to keep Helen, and to kill both the envoys; and murdered they would have been, had not Antenor saved them, and got them quickly out of the city.

When they returned to the fleet with their news, the Greeks were filled with rage at the insolence of the Trojans, and decided to land at once and teach them a sharp lesson.

So the fleet drew in towards the beach, and the Trojans came rushing down in thousands to oppose their landing. Achilles was about to leap ashore to deal the first blow in the war, but Calchas held him back:

'There is an oracle,' he cried, 'which says that the first to land is the first to be slain – and we cannot afford to lose you, son of Thetis!'

Then, while the Greeks hesitated, brave Protesilaus, son of Iphiclus the Argonaut, cried:

'Heroes of Hellas, follow me! To die in glory is to live for ever on the lips of men!'

So saying, he leapt ashore, and after slaying many Trojans, fell at the hands of mighty Hector, bravest of the sons of Priam. Over the sides of their ships poured the rest of the Greeks, and a tremendous battle was fought that day in which many fell.

For a time the Greeks were held at bay by Cycnus, the invulnerable son of Poseidon, who killed numbers of them. Achilles rushed to meet him, but found that even the spear which Chiron had cut for him could not pierce the unwoundable Cycnus. Then he slashed at him with his sword, but once more in vain.

'No weapon can pierce me!' laughed Cycnus. But even as he spoke Achilles dashed him in the face with his shield, made him give ground, and tripped him dextrously. Then he seized his fallen foe and exerting his great strength he strangled him with the straps of his own helmet. But Poseidon saw the fate of his son, and bearing his body swiftly away he turned him into a snow-white swan.

When the Trojans knew that Cycnus was slain, they fled back into Troy town and barred the gates; nor would they venture out again for many a long day.

So the Greeks made their great encampment all round the city, and laid siege to it. But Troy was so large and the Trojans, both within its walls and in the country round about, were so strong, that the Greeks could not blockade it completely, and the Trojans never suffered the full hardships of a long siege. They had plenty of water: they could always get food, and from time to time reinforcements won their way into the city.

Failing to take Troy by storm or siege, the Greeks enlivened their ten-year campaign by overrunning the country round and sacking the other cities under Trojan rule or in league with them.

The years dragged by in this way; city after city was besieged, attacked and finally destroyed, but few notable deeds were done of which any record survives.

One event which has grown with the telling concerned one of Priam's sons called Troilus. It is said that he loved the daughter of the traitor-prophet Calchas who was still in Troy, and that their love prospered, thanks to the girl's uncle, Pandarus. But Calchas, being certain that Troy would fall, persuaded Agamemnon to exchange the girl for an important prisoner. Troilus was heart-broken, but consoled himself with the vows of eternal love and faith which he and his beloved had exchanged – until he discovered that, the moment she arrived in the Greek camp, the faithless girl transferred her affections to Diomedes.

When Calchas announced that Troy would never fall if Troilus reached the age of twenty, determined efforts were made to kill him. Finally Achilles surprised him in the sanctuary of Apollo on Mount Ida, and slew him mercilessly.

Not long after this Achilles marched against Aeneas who, although he had been with Paris when Helen was carried off, had taken no part in the war. Achilles attacked his stronghold on Mount Ida, after driving away all his cattle, and Aeneas only escaped by the help of Aphrodite, and so made his way into Troy.

In the ninth year of the war, Palamedes met his end mysteriously. Though not much of a warrior, he had earned the gratitude of the Greek soldiers by inventing games for them to play during the long, weary siege – both draughts and dice were credited to his ingenious mind.

One day the dead body of a Trojan spy was discovered and on it was a letter from Priam to Palamedes saying: 'The gold which I have sent to you is the reward for betraying the Greeks to me.'

Palamedes was brought before Agamemnon, and denied having received gold from Priam, or from anyone else. But when a search was made of his tent, treasure was discovered buried under it.

That was the end of Palamedes: he was condemned to death, and was stoned or drowned when out fishing. When sentence was passed on him, he cried: 'Truth, I mourn for you: I am about to die, but you have perished before me!'

His brother Oeax believed that he was really innocent, and that Odysseus and Diomedes had forged the letter and hidden the gold, with the help of Agamemnon himself. So he sent a message to his father King Nauplius, accusing the Greek leaders of murdering Palamedes; and Nauplius, though unable to take vengeance while they were still at Troy, prepared for them an unpleasant welcome on their return to Greece.

But meanwhile, in the beginning of the tenth year of the war, a great quarrel broke out among the Greek leaders themselves, due to the pride and insolence of King Agamemnon.

Not long before, Achilles had captured two maidens named Chryseis and Briseis, the first of whom was the daughter of a priest of Apollo, and sacred to that Immortal. Agamemnon, as lord over the lesser kings of the Greek host, divided up all spoils of conquest – and usually kept the best for himself. On this occasion he gave Briseis to Achilles as a handmaiden, but kept Chryseis, and when her father came to beg him to give back the girl, drove him away with harsh and impious words.

Apollo's priest prayed to Apollo for aid, and that Immortal Lord of the Silver Bow came down in anger from Olympus and discharged several of his deadly Arrows of Pestilence into the Greek camp.

As usual when anything occurred which was obviously the work of some angered Immortal, Agamemnon and the other kings consulted Calchas, and he, having secured the protection of Achilles, turned on the 'King of Men', and declared:

'Apollo has smitten us because you, King Agamemnon, did not harken to the prayer of his priest; and will not remove this loathsome pestilence from the Greeks until you return Chryseis to her father – with a great gift as compensation.'

Agamemnon was furiously angry: 'You vile seer!' he cried. 'Never yet have you told me anything pleasant: all your prophecies are of evil, and I am the one who has to suffer for them!'

Nevertheless he was forced to give up Chryseis; but because Achilles had promised to protect Calchas from his rage, Agamemnon turned on him and took away Briseis to replace his own lost handmaiden.

Then it was Achilles who lost his temper: 'You shameless, crafty, grasping wretch!' he began. 'You dog-faced cheat! Was it for this that we followed you from Greece and have obeyed you all these years? Well, I for one have had enough of it, and I am minded to sail away with all my men and ships before you rob me of the few spoils that are still mine.'

'Flee if you like!' shouted Agamemnon. 'I will make no attempt to hinder you, nor to beg you to remain! There are many to stand by me and treat me with the honour which is my due. Go home, you coward, and lord it over your Myrmidons: I shall be well rid of you!'

Mad with rage, Achilles set his hand to his sword, meaning to draw it and slay Agamemnon there and then. But Athena was watching, and she drew near quickly, invisible to all but Achilles, and caught him by his golden hair.

'Achilles!' she said, and her eyes shone terribly. 'I come to you from the high place of the Immortals to stay your anger. Harken to me, for I am sent by Hera, the white-armed Queen of Olympus, who loves you both equally, and would not have the blood of either of you spilt in civil strife. Therefore fight only with words, if fight you must, and then retire to your tents: for I promise you that honour and good things are reserved for you in threefold measure.'

Achilles bowed to the will of the wise Immortal; but he turned upon Agamemnon and said:

'Listen, you drunken, dog-faced, deer-hearted coward, who has never once dared to lead the Greeks in battle, or to lie in ambush with the other princes of Hellas! I swear, by this staff which shall never more grow in the earth nor bring forth green leaves, that however much you may long for my aid when the Greeks fall before manslaying Hector, I will not raise a finger to help you, until my own ships are in danger!'

So Achilles retired to his tents and hung up his armour; and his cousin Patroclus did likewise, and so did all the host of the Myrmidons. But Agamemnon sent Chryseis back to her father, and took Briseis from Achilles with further insulting words.

Then Achilles called to the sea-nymph Thetis, his mother, and she came to him out of the waves, and he told her all that had happened and begged her aid.

'I will go at once to Olympus,' said Thetis, 'and pray mighty Zeus to help us. Surely he will bring it to pass that the Trojans may gain such a victory over the Greeks that Agamemnon will be forced to humble himself before you and beg your help on his knees!'

Thetis did even as she had said, and Zeus was gracious to her, and that very night he sent a deceitful dream to Agamemnon. And that dream took the shape of old Nestor, wisest of the Greeks, whose advice Agamemnon was always ready to take.

'Rise, King of Men,' cried the Dream, disguised in the likeness of King Nestor, 'I come as a messenger from Zeus himself. The Immortals have been swayed by the counsel of Queen Hera, and if you lead the Greeks in full force against Troy this day, you will take the city and level its walls with the ground . . . Keep this in your heart and forget not my words when you awake – for they are words of truth!'

Agamemnon woke rejoicing, called together the leaders of the Greeks and told them of his dream. They believed it also, and, arming themselves, marched out to do battle with the Trojans.

Meanwhile the news of Agamemnon's quarrel with Achilles had been brought to Troy, and the Trojans themselves decided to march out and scatter the Greeks while their most mighty warrior was sulking in his tent.

So the two armies met on the level plain outside Troy; and Paris, seized with unexpected boldness, offered to meet Menelaus in single combat.

'If I slay you,' he said, 'then the Greeks must swear to return home without Helen. But if I fall, Helen shall be returned, and a great treasure besides.'

The Greeks, who were heartily sick of the war,

agreed eagerly to this, and both sides swore to keep the truce and to abide by the outcome of the battle between Menelaus and Paris.

When she heard of what was about to happen, Helen came hastening to the wall above the scene of the single combat. And Priam, who was there to see it also, exclaimed at the sight of her amazing beauty:

'Small wonder is it that Trojans and Greeks should endure long hardships and battles for such a woman – for indeed she is marvellously like to one of the Immortals in her very loveliness!'

But Helen sighed, and made answer: 'Would that sore death had come to me before ever your son Paris led me away from happy Sparta and my dear daughter Hermione. Alas, my lord Menelaus must think me the most shameful of all women!'

Menelaus, however, was preparing to do battle for Helen as if she had been as perfect a bride as Alcestis was to Admetus; and Paris was doing the same, as if she had been his lawfully wedded wife, and as though there were no deserted woodnymph Oenone pining in tears on lonely Ida.

First each of the heroes set the greaves upon his legs, beautifully fashioned and fastened with silver ankle-clasps; next upon his chest each fastened the moulded corselet of beaten bronze; and over his shoulder cast the baldric which held his brazen sword with the silver-studded handle. And on his mighty head each set a cunningly wrought helmet with a great crest of horse-hair that nodded

terribly, and took in his hand a strong ashen spear
with a point of bronze.

So, when they had armed themselves, they stood
forth between the ranks of Trojans and Greeks,
who sat in their long lines to watch the battle.

It smote the round shield of Paris and passed through it

First Paris hurled his spear and smote Menelaus
on the shield, but the point was turned and did
not pierce it. Then Menelaus, uttering a prayer to
Zeus, threw his weapon. It smote the round shield
of Paris, and passed through it – so mightily did he
cast in his anger. It pierced the wrought breast-

plate also, and Paris would have died then and there had he not managed to twist away so that the blade did but graze his side.

Menelaus flung down his shield with a cry of triumph, and leaping forward seized Paris by his horse-hair crest, and swinging him round, dragged him by the head towards the Grecian lines. And Paris would have been strangled like Cycnus by the straps of his own helmet, if Aphrodite had not come to his aid. But she snapped the straps suddenly, so that Menelaus rolled over backwards, holding the empty helmet in his hands, and when he leapt to his feet – Paris was gone. For Paris was no longer the brave young herdsman of Ida: rather than feats of strength and daring, he preferred to dally away the hours with his unwilling bride. Now, shielded by Aphrodite, he fled swiftly back to Troy, and hid himself in Helen's bower.

But Menelaus, failing to find him, marched proudly up and down between the armies, shouting:

'Harken to me, Trojans and Greeks! Paris has fled, and the victory is mine! Therefore Helen is mine! Give her back to me, and we will sail away and trouble Troy no more!'

All the Greeks and Trojans agreed with this, and a cry of joy went up from either side, for the war was over, and they could go home in peace!

CHAPTER 6

THE ADVENTURE OF RHESUS

*

What eyes, what ears hath sweet Andromache,
  Save for her Hector's form and step; as tear
    On tear made salt the warm last kiss he gave?
He goes. Cassandra's words beat heavily
  Like crows above his crest, and at his ear
    Ring hollow in the shield that shall not save.

ROSSETTI
Cassandra

CHAPTER SIX

THIS would indeed have been the end of the War, had it not been for the treachery of the Trojan Pandarus. For when he saw Menelaus striding boastfully up and down and taunting Paris for running away, he fitted a sharp arrow to his polished bow of ibex horn, and loosed a shaft which wounded Menelaus in the side, just where he had wounded Paris with his spear.

At this cries of rage and scorn rose from the Greeks: 'Now we will smite the Trojans!' they cried. 'For they have broken the truce, and Zeus will surely be on our side!'

They armed in haste, and the Trojans did the same, and both sides rushed together and engaged in the hottest battle there had been since the very beginning when the Greeks first landed on Trojan soil and brave Protesilaus was slain. The noise of shield meeting shield was like the roar of a mountain torrent at mid-winter; and when a man fell he was stripped of his armour and trodden underfoot.

Many deeds were done in that battle of which the minstrels sang in after days. They told how Menelaus slew fierce Scamandrius, the mighty hunter; how Diomedes fought with Aeneas and would have slain him had not Aphrodite come to her son's aid, and suffered a wound herself, Immortal though she was. They told also of the mighty doings of Odysseus who ranged through the cowering Trojans like a wolf in a sheep-fold.

While this great battle was raging, and the Trojans were getting the worst of it, their great champion Hector was in Troy, searching angrily for Paris. He found him at last in Helen's room, and she was weeping and calling him a coward:

'Would that the winds had wafted me away, and that the waves had drowned me before ever I came to Troy with such a one as you!' she cried.

Paris hung his head, and made excuses, and at last consented to re-arm and go down into the battle.

Then, leaving his cowardly brother reluctantly buckling on his armour, Hector strode away to his own house; and there he found his beloved wife Andromache, nursing their little golden-haired son Astyanax, beautiful as a star.

'My dear lord,' said Andromache, weeping softly, 'do not go out to battle this day, for I fear greatly lest you should be slain. My father was killed by Achilles in the beginning of this dreadful war, and if you fall, Troy will fall also. So do not go to the battle, but stay here with us; for if Troy falls, I shall be sold into slavery – and our son they will surely slay, child though he be, lest he grow up to avenge your death upon their children.'

But Hector made answer: 'Indeed I think of all these things, dearest wife, but if I held back from the battle I would never again be able to hold up my head before the men and women of Troy. I fear that Troy is indeed doomed, and that it will soon be laid low and its people slain or sold into slavery. But let me fall honourably in battle – for death is better than shame, and how could I endure to see you led away captive.'

So spoke Hector, and stretched out his arms to

Hector . . . stretched out his arms to Astyanax, but the child shrank away crying

Astyanax. But the child shrank away crying, afraid of the great nodding crest on his father's helmet. Then Hector laughed, and Andromache also, and he took off his helmet and laid it on the ground, and lifted the child and dandled him in his arms, saying:

'Now I pray to Zeus, and to all the Immortals, that my son may grow up to be as valiant as I am, and a mighty king of Troy. May people say, when they see him return victorious from battle, "Far greater is he than ever his father was!" And may he live long to gladden your heart when I am no more.'

So saying he placed the child in its mother's arms, and kissed and comforted her: 'Dearest, do not sorrow over much,' he said, 'no man may escape his fate, be he coward or hero.'

Then he went swiftly to the battle, while Andromache wept and would not be comforted; for she was certain that they had said their last farewell.

Down on the battle field Hector rallied the Trojan ranks with such good effect that presently it was the Greeks who were retreating. Then he cried aloud a challenge:

'Come forth and do battle with me, man to man, who ever is bravest and most daring among the Greeks! I am not Paris, but Hector – and Hector will not run away!'

This challenge was meant for Achilles who was still sulking in his tent, but he would not come, even to show his strength against Hector. But many of the Greek leaders sprang forward as volunteers – Agamemnon among them, and Diomedes, Ajax and Odysseus, and more besides. Then at Nestor's suggestion they cast lots in a helmet, and that of Ajax first fell to the ground.

So Ajax stepped forward in his flashing bronze,

the biggest man among all the Greeks, looking as fierce and as mighty as Ares the Immortal War-lord himself.

'Now, Hector!' cried he exultantly. 'Come and fight me if you dare! I'll show you what men there are among the Greeks, even though Achilles is not with us today.'

The two champions attacked each other with spear and sword, and many were the blows dealt and guarded. But neither could win the advantage, and soon darkness began to fall, and the heralds cried a truce. As night came on, the warriors drew apart, and exchanged gifts – one worthy foeman with another.

That night the Greeks laboured without ceasing and made a wall and a ditch to protect themselves and the ships from the Trojans. In the morning the battle was resumed with even greater fury, and the Greeks were driven back behind their new wall.

As for the Trojans, they camped out in the plain and did not bother to return for safety to their city, but sat about their camp-fires singing and rejoicing in their victory, feeling certain that next day they would conquer the Greeks and burn all their ships.

But in the Grecian camp the leaders sat in council together with long faces and troubled hearts.

And first Agamemnon spoke, saying:

'My friends, leaders and captains of the host, surely Zeus has smitten us this day, and there can be only one meaning in what he has done, that we shall never conquer Troy. Therefore let us flee swiftly while yet the ships remain to us, and return home to our own land.'

'Go if you like, coward king!' cried Diomedes at this. 'But I at least will stay and fight it out!'

The other kings applauded him, and Nestor advised that first of all a good watch should be kept along the wall lest the Trojans planned a night attack. So Diomedes, with five hundred men under Nestor's son Thrasymedes went to see to this important task, while Nestor went on:

'Most noble Agamemnon, king of men, all this woe comes of your folly in robbing Achilles of the girl Briseis. You know well that without him we cannot conquer Hector nor take Troy. Therefore my counsel is that you swallow your pride and send to Achilles offering him back the girl, with many fair gifts, if only he will pardon the insult which you did him and return to the war.'

'Wise Nestor,' answered Agamemnon, 'I was indeed a fool, and I readily admit my folly. I will send Odysseus and brave Ajax to Achilles with such a message as you suggest; and they must promise him Briseis, and twenty Trojan maidens, besides a ship load of gold and bronze. If these will not suffice, he shall have his choice of one of my daughters to be his wife, when we return from conquered Troy.'

Off went the two kings on this errand, but even the persuasive speech of Odysseus could not move Achilles, who only smiled grimly and answered:

'My advice is for us all to return speedily to Greece. You cannot conquer Troy without my aid – and I am minded to withhold that aid, and so save the life which otherwise I am fated to lose. I sail home in the morning.'

When Agamemnon heard this, he wept and tore his hair. But Nestor strove to encourage him, Menelaus saying:

'We must prepare for tomorrow's battle. Is there anyone who will dare to go secretly among the Trojans and spy out their camp – and perhaps overhear their counsel?'

'That will I!' cried Odysseus, and Diomedes volunteering to go with him, the two set out, wearing leather caps and no armour, but taking their swords.

Meanwhile the Trojans had hit upon the same idea, and a young man named Dolon had volunteered to spy for them if Priam would promise him the magic horses of Achilles – Poseidon's wedding-present to Peleus and Thetis – as a reward.

This was agreed and he went out into the night, wearing a grey wolf skin over his shoulders and carrying his bow in his hand.

When Odysseus and Diomedes saw him coming, they lay down quickly among the dead, and pretended to be corpses also. But as soon as he had passed, they sprang up and seized hold of him from behind.

'Do not kill me!' begged Dolon, green with fear. 'My father is very rich, and will pay a vast ransom for my life. Moreover, I will give you news of the Trojans – anything, if only you will spare me!'

'Speak swiftly!' said Odysseus, and the wretched youth began to tell them about the Trojans plans for the morrow.

'But what you should do,' he babbled, 'is to steal away the horses of King Rhesus. He arrived this evening from Thrace with all his men, and there is a prophecy that Troy will never fall if once his wonderful white horses have entered the city. Now send me, a prisoner to the ships, and if I have spoken truly, set me free and my father will pay ransom.'

'Not so,' answered Diomedes, 'a spy and a traitor is not fit to live!' And with that he smote off the wretched Dolon's head.

Then he and Odysseus stole on through the darkness, and soon came to the place where the newly arrived Thracians were camped. Here they slew several men in their sleep, including the unfortunate King Rhesus himself. Then they loosed the horses, tied them together, and Diomedes drove them carefully between the sleeping men, and away towards the Greek camp.

But presently a Thracian woke suddenly, and when he saw dead men lie bleeding on the ground and the white horses gone, he cried aloud, and his comrades leapt to their feet, snatching up their swords.

Then Diomedes leapt upon the back of the nearest horse and galloped away until he came to the tent of Agamemnon. But Odysseus remained among the Thracians, in deadly peril, and indeed he was soon surrounded by them.

'Here's the man who killed our king!' shouted a Thracian captain.

'Fool!' cried Odysseus in a voice of authority. 'You'll suffer for this if you are not careful!'

'Then give the watchword,' persisted the Captain, 'or I'll drive my spear into you!'

'The watchword is "Phoebus",' answered Odysseus quietly, having had the foresight to learn it from Dolon.

'Right!' cried the Captain, letting go of him. 'Do you know which way the murderer went?'

'Of course I do,' answered Odysseus angrily, 'I was pursuing him when you were fool enough to stop me! Come along with me!'

With that he set off at his best speed and was soon back in the Greek camp, while the Thracians were receiving a warm welcome from Thrasymedes and his five hundred guards on the wall.

CHAPTER 7

THE DEATH OF HECTOR

*

But one that was my comfort and my joy,
Hector, the very pride and prop of Troy,
One that the bulwark of his brethren was,
Him hast thou slain, and I am left alone!

HOMER
The Iliad (Translated by Andrew Lang)

CHAPTER SEVEN

DAWNING day brought a mass attack from the Trojans, furious at the death of King Rhesus and the theft of his white horses. The Greeks, encouraged by the exploits of Diomedes and Odysseus, met them fiercely, led by Ajax; and one of the greatest battles of the Trojan War began.

At first the Greeks had the better of it, as Hector was not fighting in the Trojan vanguard but marshalling his troops from behind. Agamemnon, putting from him his usual cowardice, led his army to such good effect that the Trojans at last broke and fled back towards their city. But near the gates Hector rallied them, and Agamemnon was wounded by the spear of a Thracian captain, and carried back to the ships in his chariot. Then Hector charged at the head of the Trojans, and the Greeks fled before him. Near the encampment Diomedes and Odysseus turned at bay, and held off the pursuers while the Greeks reformed their ranks.

Then Hector led another charge, but Diomedes took good aim with his mighty spear and struck him on the helmet. The spear did not pierce it, but so heavy was the blow that Hector fell stunned to the earth, and was carried out of the battle in his chariot.

Diomedes was shot through the foot by Paris shortly after, so he was also out of the battle, leaving Odysseus to rally the front ranks. Long he fought there and slew many Trojans, but at last a spear pierced his shield and bit deep into his side. With a cry he plucked it out and with it slew the man who had wounded him: then, as he sank to the ground he called aloud to Ajax and Menelaus, who rushed forward to the rescue. Ajax with his great shield protected Odysseus while he climbed into a chariot, and then Menelaus drove him back to the ships to have his wound dressed.

While Ajax was doing great deeds and keeping back the advancing Trojans, the wounded kings were holding a hurried conference beside the ships.

'The only thing to do is to keep them off until night, and then launch our ships quietly and escape!' urged Agamemnon.

But Odysseus turned on him fiercely: 'You should be leading some band of common cowards,' he cried, 'not the army of the Greeks! We will fight, every one of us, and perish to a man rather than run away. Be silent, if you have no other advice to give, for it would be shameful if the common soldiers heard the King of Men utter such cowardly words.'

Agamemnon, shamed once more into courage, urged the Greeks to make another charge, and Ajax led them as bravely as ever. Meeting Hector, he smote him with a great stone, so that he was carried away bleeding at the mouth. The tide of battle turned then for a while and the Trojans retreated; but when Hector had recovered he led such a charge, with Paris on one side of him and

'The ships are on fire and most of the Greek kings wounded . . .'

Aeneas on the other, that the Greeks fled in good earnest.

'To the ships! To the ships!' cried Hector. 'Burn the ships so that they cannot get away! Time for spoils when the battle is over! Burn the ships first!'

They were fighting now on the very sea-shore, and Ajax was aboard his own ship wielding a great spear which was kept for repelling boarders in a sea-fight. Twelve men who tried to set fire to his ship were slain by him; but he could not guard all the ships, and presently Hector himself flung a torch on to the one from which brave Protesilaus had leapt to his death at the beginning of the war.

But help came unexpectedly. Patroclus, cousin of Achilles, had been tending a wounded friend, but when he saw that the Trojans were trying to burn the ships, he rushed off to Achilles.

'If you will not fight,' he cried, 'at least let me lead our Myrmidons to battle! The ships are on fire and most of the Greek kings wounded.'

Then Achilles was sorry that, in his anger, he had sworn not to fight until his own ships were in danger. But he bade Patroclus wear his own armour so that the Trojans should think that Achilles himself was leading the Myrmidons, and urged him forth before it was too late.

Meanwhile Ajax fought fiercely on; but he was growing weary and could hardly hold up the great spear any longer. Then Hector attacked him, and cut off the spear's brazen point with a blow of his sword. Ajax drew back, and a moment later his ship was ablaze.

Just at that critical moment there rose a cry of fear from the Trojans, and they fell back hurriedly shouting:

'Achilles! Achilles the invincible comes against us once more!'

And there was Patroclus, in the shining armour which all knew so well, and drawn in the chariot by the two magic horses which Poseidon had given to Peleus. Straight to the ships he went, and quenched the flames which were destroying the ship of Protesilaus. Then he turned the chariot and led the whole Greek army in a tremendous charge against the Trojans who fled in disorder across the ditch and over the wide plain towards the city of Troy.

For a while the flight was stayed by King Sarpedon of Lycia, an ally of the Trojans. He engaged with Patroclus and a fierce combat ensued. Patroclus struck the first blow, but his dart went wide and transfixed the charioteer. Sarpedon retaliated with two darts, one after the other, but in his over-eagerness he missed his aim with both. Then Patroclus launched a spear with all his strength and it pierced Sarpedon so that he fell like a tall tree smitten down on the hillside by the sharp axe of the woodman.

But as he lay dying he cried out:

'Fight on, brave Lycians! Do not fly because I am down! Rescue my body from the Greeks to give it worthy funeral!'

Fiercely the fight raged over his dead body, but in the end the Greeks tore the armour from him.

Yet Apollo, pitying the fallen champion, sent out Sleep and Death, and they carried away the body, over land and sea to Lycia, there to be laid quietly to rest.

But Patroclus pursued the flying Trojans right to the very walls of Troy, and strove even to enter, but was pushed back three times. Then Hector came thundering out of the gateway in his chariot, mowing down all who came in his way, and drove straight at Patroclus – who flung a heavy stone at him, missed his mark, but killed the charioteer. For a few minutes the two heroes struggled over the body of the slain man, and then the surge of battle parted them.

The sun was sinking when they met again, and Patroclus had lost his helmet in the thick of the battle, and was weary and wounded. Nevertheless he charged at Hector, who met him in full career and transfixed his body with a spear. Then Patroclus fell to the ground, and as Hector stood over him with drawn sword, he gasped:

'Do not boast greatly at my slaying, noble Hector – for stern fate decreed it – fate that no man may escape. And know that you yourself have not long to live, for already Death is on his way from the realm of Hades: and by the hand of great Achilles shall you fall!'

Then Patroclus died, and his charioteer sped like the wind out of the rush of battle, drawn by the two magic horses, and brought the news to Achilles as he sat alone in his tent.

When Achilles heard that his beloved cousin

was dead, he covered his face with his hands and wept. By and by, as he still sat there alone, his mother the sea-nymph Thetis came to him, and for a long time she strove in vain to comfort him.

'Let me die, let me die!' groaned Achilles, 'since I might not save my friend from death, and through my foolish anger he is dead . . . All I ask is to slay Hector who has done this thing!'

Then, unarmed as he was, Achilles rushed out of his tent and on to the wall of the camp. There he stood, tall and godlike, with the red sunset blazing behind him. Down on the plain he saw the battle raging fiercely. He saw that Hector had stripped the armour from dead Patroclus – the golden armour which the Immortals had given to Peleus – and that the Greeks, still led by Ajax, were fighting to bring the poor, maimed, naked body of the dead hero back into their camp.

Achilles saw, and he uttered his mighty voice in a cry which rang like a clarion call over the field of battle: and the thunder rolling on Mount Ida seemed to be but the echo of that cry. Thrice Achilles uttered that terrible cry, and the Trojans drew back in fear, while the very horses snorted and shied away.

Then the Greeks took up the body of Patroclus and bore it back to the camp; and as they did so, night fell.

Once more the Trojans camped on the open plain, and Hector would not return to Troy, though his friends warned him that Achilles would never rest now until one or the other lay dead.

'Never will I flee!' he cried. 'What though the great Achilles come against me? One of us must fall – but Ares the Immortal Warlord may guide my spear so that Achilles is the one who dies!'

But Achilles rested in his tent, grieving over the loss of Patroclus; and presently, by the will of the Immortals, sweet sleep came to him and he was at rest. There was no rest in the forge of Hephaestus the Immortal Smith that night, however: for at the prayer of Thetis he was forging new armour for Achilles.

In the grey morning Thetis, the sea-nymph, came down from high Olympus bearing the wonderful armour for her son – a five-fold shield tooled and engraved all over with scenes and devices; a corselet brighter than a flame of fire, a massive helmet with its golden crest, and greaves of pliant tin.

Achilles beheld these wondrous things, and his eyes glittered with delight. Swiftly he put them on and took a great spear in his hand. Then he went down by the shore, crying his terrible cry, and all the Grecian warriors sprang up from sleep, buckled on their armour and made ready for battle.

But first Odysseus came to Achilles and persuaded him to visit the wounded Agamemnon, to receive his apologies and the gifts which were to be made him.

Peace restored between the kings, Achilles went forth to war in his brazen chariot drawn by the two magic horses. And as he was tightening the harness on their backs, one of them spoke to him in a human voice, saying: 'We shall bear you swiftly and speedily: but your day of death is near – death that will come to you in battle.'

'Well do I know it,' answered Achilles, 'but I shall not cease from fighting until that day, unless I may lay proud Troy in the dust.'

All day long the battle raged, and the Trojans fled before the wrath of Achilles, leaving many, many dead upon the field. Across the River Scamander he drove them, and did not pause, though the River rose against him in an angry flood. Over the plain fled the Trojans, with Achilles hot at their heels, and they did not pause from flight until they were safe behind the walls of Troy.

But Hector alone stood at the Scaean Gate of the city, waiting for Achilles who came rushing on, shining like a shooting-star in his golden armour.

'Come within the gate!' cried King Priam. 'This terrible man has slain many of my sons, and if he slays you also, who shall I have to help me in my old age?'

But Hector would not listen, and he went forth to meet Achilles, leaving Priam and Hecuba on the towers over the gate with Andromache and the other Trojan wives. They met near where a spring still bubbles out of the plain by a little grove of trees, and as they fought they moved out of sight round a corner of the city walls.

Achilles hurled his spear and missed Hector, who in his turn hurled his own weapon which failed to pierce the wondrous shield. Then Hector drew his sword, but Achilles had a second spear and caught him on the point of it as he rushed against him.

Hector fell in the dust, and Achilles cried: 'Slayer of Patroclus, dogs and birds shall tear your flesh as you lie unburied!'

'Do not do this great shame!' gasped Hector. 'Take the store of gold my father will offer you, and let my body be burnt in Troy!'

'Hound, even if Priam offered me your weight in gold, I doubt if it would save your corpse from the dogs!' shouted vengeful Achilles.

'Remember me in the day when Paris slays you in the Scaean Gate!' said Hector quietly, and with that he fell back dead.

Then Achilles pierced his feet, and having stripped him, tied him to the back of his chariot and drove in triumph round and round the walls of Troy, while Andromache shrieked and fainted, and Priam and all the Trojans wept.

Next day Achilles burned the body of Patroclus on a great funeral pyre, and sacrificed twelve prisoners of war to his ghost – a deed of shame which caused great Zeus to turn away his eyes. And he caused games to be held in honour of Patroclus, and all the Greek kings took part in them.

And each day he trailed the body of Hector round the walls of Troy, until the Immortals grew angry, and sent Thetis to tell her son that he must render up the body for an honourable funeral.

For without the rites of fire, the Greeks and Trojans believed that no spirit could depart into the Kingdom of Hades through which all must pass, even if they were fated to dwell in the Isles of the Blest and the sweet Elysian Fields.

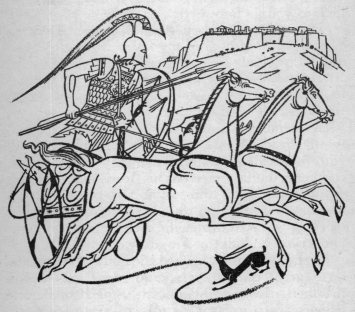

And each day he trailed the body of Hector round the walls of Troy

That night King Priam came through the ranks of the Greeks to the very tent of Achilles, and kneeling at his feet he kissed the terrible hands which had slain his son and wept silently.

Then Achilles remembered his old father Peleus,

waiting alone in distant Hellas, and he wept also and raised the sorrowing king with gentle words, gave him food and drink and sent him back to Troy with all honour.

In the morning he bade Briseis and the other hand-maidens wash the body of Hector and clothe it in fair linen.

Then he set up a great pair of scales under the walls of Troy and placed the body in one pan: for he had sworn only to give up the corpse of Hector in exchange for his weight in gold.

But when Priam had stripped his treasury to make up the weight, the scale still trembled and would not turn, till Hector's lovely sister Polyxena, youngest of Priam's children, leant over the wall and cast her golden bracelets into the scale, then Hector's body rose as the weight of gold sank to the ground.

So they carried Hector into Troy, amidst great lamentations and, bending over him, fair Helen cried:

'Hector, of all my brethren in Troy the dearest, since Paris brought me here – but would that I had died ere ever that day dawned. Hector, in all the years since then I have never heard from you a word that was bitter or unkind. Others spoke cruelly to me, for whom this bitter war is fought: but ever you would restrain them with gentle, courteous words. Ah woe is me! Woe is me! Now there is none like you left in all Troy, and my one true friend is dead.'

CHAPTER 8

NEOPTOLEMUS AND PHILOCTETES

*

Yet is there hope; slow hope yet comfort sure,
I had forgot it in my wrath and pain.
Is there no oracle? Troy cannot fall.
I guard thine arrows, Heracles divine,
And Troy falls not without them.

LORD DE TABLEY
Philoctetes

CHAPTER EIGHT

THE Trojan War did not end with the death of Hector, but now the Trojans ventured out into the open less and less often, while the Greeks besieged them even more closely than before.

Yet, though all the lesser cities lay waste far and wide, the Trojans still had allies: and the first of these that came to their aid after the death of Hector was the beautiful Penthesilia, Queen of the Amazons.

The Trojans sallied out to battle when they saw her coming, but Achilles drove them back again, and turned against Penthesilia. Their meeting was sharp and brief, for Achilles pierced her with his spear and she fell dying to the ground. As he bent over her to strip off her armour, he realized for the first time that he had slain a lovely girl. Then his heart was stirred with regret at the thought that he might instead have captured her and carried her away to be his slave-wife – or even his queen, if Deidamia were dead; and he mourned his unlucky stroke with tears, for indeed the lovely Amazon was divinely fair and like one of the Immortals, since her father was Ares the Warlord.

Then Thersites, the ugliest and vilest of the Greeks, jeered at Achilles:

'Yah, sorry-souled Achilles! It only needs a pretty face to turn you from a warrior into a womanish traitor worse than Paris himself! As for this dirty Amazon slut, she's only good for dogs' meat!' And with that he began jabbing at the corpse with his spear.

Then Achilles lost his temper completely: 'Take that, shameless wretch!' he shouted, 'No man shall revile Achilles and go unpunished!' and he struck Thersites such a blow on the side of his head that his teeth were scattered on the ground and he fell upon his face and died.

Having slain a Greek of noble birth (for Thersites, for all his vileness, was cousin to Diomedes), Achilles needed to be cleared of blood-guilt, and sailed away to the island of Lesbos for this purpose.

While he was away, Priam's last ally arrived with an army. This was Prince Memnon of Ethiopia, son of Eos the Dawn-Titan and her mortal husband King Tithonus. The story of these two was very sad: for Eos when she fell in love with Tithonus, the most handsome of mortal men, prayed Zeus to grant that he should never die. Zeus granted this prayer without a moment's thought, and all seemed well. But Eos realized too late that, though Tithonus could never die, he could still grow old. For in time he grew so ancient that he was no more than a little shrunken, chirping creature like a large grasshopper, who could not see nor hear, but merely sit gibbering and chattering to himself, locked far away from sight in a room in the golden palace of Immortal Eos.

Strong Memnon, however, came to Troy with his swarthy followers, and once more the Trojans ventured out of their city, and together they chased the Greeks for the last time down almost to their ships. Night fell just as Ajax was preparing to go out against Memnon; and in the morning Achilles returned from Lesbos and turned the tide of battle, slaying the Ethiopian King and scattering his forces. Then he chased the Trojans helter-skelter across the plain and into Troy, mocking them and boasting that even the Immortals would not be able to withstand him, if he came in arms against them.

But as he stood there in the Scaean Gate, Paris took an arrow from his quiver, set it to his bow, took careful aim and loosed. Away sped the shaft, guided by Apollo who was angry at Achilles's words. It struck him in the heel – the one vulnerable part of his whole body – the heel by which Thetis had held him when she dipped him as a baby in the River Styx.

The arrow was poisoned, and presently Achilles fell to the ground with a great cry, and died.

For a little while friend and foe stood staring, and aghast, for neither could believe that so great a hero could really be dead. Then, with a shout of triumph, the Trojans rushed forward to spoil the body: but mighty Ajax seized it, swung it over his shoulders and raced for the ships with it, never heeding the shower of darts which were sped after him.

Mad with rage and grief the Greeks, headed by Odysseus, drove the Trojans back into Troy, and invested the city more mercilessly than ever. Next day they burnt the body of Achilles on a great pyre, and buried his ashes with those of Patroclus on the sea-coast and heaped a great mound over them which is there to this day. But Thetis snatched away the soul of her son and took him to the Isles of the Blest reserved for the spirits of the heroes.

Once again, the Greeks did honour to a dead hero by holding games; and at the close of them Agamemnon rashly said that he would give the armour of Achilles to the bravest of the Greeks.

At once quarrels arose as to who could claim that honour. Agamemnon favoured his brother Menelaus, but the general vote placed the contest between Ajax and Odysseus. No one dared to decide which of the two had the best claim, and the argument grew more and more heated.

At last wise old Nestor exclaimed: 'Friends, we cannot settle this question ourselves – but why should not the Trojans decide it for us? Send spies quickly to Troy: let them listen under the walls and tell us what the Trojans think of our two great heroes – who to me seem absolutely equal in courage!'

Everyone praised the wisdom of Nestor's suggestion, and the spies were sent accordingly. Presently one returned, and said:

'My lords, as we listened beneath the walls we heard the women of Troy speaking above us. One said: "Ajax is the bravest of the Greeks! Why, he carried the body of Achilles out of the battle, which even Odysseus did not dare to do!" But another answered her: "What nonsense you do talk! Even a woman could have carried him away, if some-

body put him on her back: but she could not fight
as Odysseus did – she would faint with fear if it
came to fighting!"'

Even this was not quite conclusive, but a secret
vote among the Greek kings showed that most of
them considered Odysseus to be the victor.

Hearing this, Ajax turned without a word and
strode blindly to his tent so dazed with grief and
fury that presently his mind gave way and a bout
of madness descended upon him. In his frenzy he
imagined that Agamemnon and Menelaus had
cheated him and given the armour to Odysseus just
to insult him; and he rose up in the darkness and
set out with drawn sword to slay all three of them
in their sleep.

Athena, however, was watchful that night, and
knowing what Ajax was minded to do, she led him
astray in the darkness so that he stumbled among
the flocks of sheep and began slaughtering them,
thinking they were his enemies. He even took
two rams to his tent, tied them to the pole, and
scourged them with a great whip, under the im-
pression that he was beating Agamemnon and
Menelaus to death.

In the morning he recovered his senses, and was
filled with such shame, both at his childish anger
and his murderous madness, that he went away to
a lonely part of the sea-shore and there flung himself upon his sword.

When the Greeks found what had happened
they mourned him sadly, and none was so filled
with grief as Odysseus, who vowed immediately to

give up the armour to Neoptolemus the son of Achilles as soon as he was old enough to wear it.

Ajax was buried in a stone coffin, amidst the lamentations of the Greeks: as he had not fallen in battle he could not be burnt on a pyre like the other heroes.

When the funeral was over a fresh council was called and Agamemnon spoke angrily to Calchas:

'The ten years are up!' he cried. 'You said it would be ten years before Troy fell – and Troy still stands. Now we have lost Achilles and Ajax: how can we conquer Troy?'

'You have neglected one of my earliest prophecies,' answered Calchas, who never failed of a ready reply: 'Troy cannot be conquered unless you have the arrows of Heracles to use: for by one of them Paris is fated to die. And the son of Achilles must go up against Troy, which cannot fall until he comes against it.'

Then the Greeks cheered, eager to see these prophecies fulfilled and the war ended at last; and they chose Odysseus and Diomedes, who ten years before had been to Scyros for Achilles, and bade them draw out a swift ship and bring back his son Neoptolemus.

Over the waves went the two heroes and came safely to Scyros. They drew the ship to shore and went striding up to the palace of old King Lycomedes. There in the morning light they saw Neoptolemus, still only a boy, yet tall and strong and wondrous like his father, driving his chariot and practising with spear and dart.

The boy welcomed them eagerly, and his eyes flashed with excitement when they told him the reason for their coming:

'Come to Troy!' urged Odysseus. 'We cannot take the city without you, now that your noble father Achilles is dead. All of us will welcome you with many gifts: for a start you shall have your father's golden armour as a gift from me – armour that the Warlord Ares would be proud to wear, since Immortal hands fashioned it. And when the war is won and we return to Greece, Menelaus will give you his lovely daughter Hermione to be your bride.'

Neoptolemus needed no bribes to make him eager to set out for Troy; and set out he did, in spite of the tears and prayers of his mother Deidamia, who feared greatly that she would lose her son as she had lost her husband. But sea-nymph Thetis rejoiced, knowing that her grandson went to win glory, not death at Troy; and she made no attempt to stop him as she had tried to stop Achilles.

Once more the swift ship sped over the blue Aegean: but it did not make straight for Troy. Instead, Odysseus guided it to rugged Lemnos where Philoctetes had been marooned on account of his terrible snake-bite, hid it in a deep bay, and went ashore with only Neoptolemus and a few sailors. On the way Odysseus told his young companion about Philoctetes and how he had been left there ten years before, with only the bow and arrows of Heracles.

'We can only catch him by guile,' ended Odysseus, 'and that is where you come in. If he sees me, he'll shoot: and there is no cure for the Hydra poison. So you must pretend to have quarrelled with the Greek kings, and with me in particular: say I refused to give you your father's armour. Anyhow, pretend that you left the war in a fury and, on your way home to Greece, have come to rescue him and take him with you. Once he is on the ship we can easily get the bow and arrows from him.'

Neoptolemus did not much like this kind of trickery, but he consented to do as Odysseus said, and went off by himself towards the rocky hillside where it seemed probable that Philoctetes would have found a cave in which to live. There he found the wretched man, with tangled hair and beard, dwelling in a cave with two entrances to guard against surprise, and living precariously on such game as he could shoot with his bow – which never left his hand, waking or asleep.

It was easy to make friends with the poor castaway, and very soon he was treating Neoptolemus like a son; and Neoptolemus was feeling more and more ashamed of the part which he was playing.

Presently one of the sailors arrived, pretending to be a merchant newly come from Troy, and warned Philoctetes that he was in danger:

'Odysseus and Diomedes are coming,' he cried. 'They have sworn to carry you off by force!'

Then Philoctetes hesitated no longer: 'I will

accompany you, son of Achilles!' he exclaimed. 'Take me away quickly before Odysseus comes!'

On the way to the shore Philoctetes was seized with a terrible spasm of the pain from his snake-bite. 'Hold the bow and arrows!' he gasped to

Sadly and bitterly he limped away to his cave

Neoptolemus, 'and be ready to shoot if Odysseus arrives before my fit has passed . . . . You see how I trust you: no one else has ever held the bow of Heracles except my father Poeas and myself.'

Then Philoctetes rolled on the ground in his agony and at length fainted with the pain.

When he recovered, Odysseus stood above him, and Philoctetes knew that he had been tricked. Sadly and bitterly he limped away to his cave to gather his few possessions, while Odysseus set out for the ship to send back men to bring him.

But when he returned it was to find that Neoptolemus had been overcome by his natural sense of honour and decency.

'Philoctetes,' he said, 'I cannot cheat you like this. Here are the bow and arrows: I beg you not to use them against us, even against Odysseus. What he has done is only for the good of our armies at Troy . . .'

Odysseus, returning at that moment, frankly confessed the whole scheme and begged Philoctetes to come with them of his own accord – to be received with all honour.

'I did wrong,' he said. 'First, when I marooned you here at the command of Agamemnon, and now when I sought to take you by guile.'

Philoctetes was so far moved that he made no attempt to shoot Odysseus, as he could easily have done: but he still refused to accompany him to Troy. Neoptolemus was ready to abide by his promise and take him back to Greece; and Odysseus said sadly:

'Then I must return to our friends having failed in my task. Troy cannot fall unless you two are with us!'

On a sudden, even as he spoke, Heracles, now an Immortal dwelling in the golden halls of Olympus, came down to Lemnos.

'Philoctetes!' he cried in his great voice. 'Listen, it is I, Heracles, come down from my high seat to tell you the will of Zeus. You must not return yet to Greece, but hasten to Troy with the son of Achilles. There you will be cured of your sickness and win glory as great as that of any hero. For you are now the chosen champion of that great army: seek out Paris, cause of all this evil, and strike him down with these arrows that once were mine. With them I destroyed Troy: and now for a second time Troy must fall before them.'

'It is the voice I have so often longed to hear,' whispered Philoctetes, 'the face even as I once knew it, but now divine. Indeed I shall not disobey.'

'Nor I,' echoed Neoptolemus.

'Then make haste!' cried Heracles. 'The wind is fair, and Troy is ripe to fall!'

Then Heracles went back to Olympus where the Immortals dwell. But Philoctetes, Neoptolemus and Odysseus clasped hands in token of friendship, and set sail for Troy – where Machaon, son of the Immortal Physician, Asclepius, waited to cure the ten year old snake-bite so that Philoctetes could once more take his place among the warrior kings of Greece.

CHAPTER 9

THE THEFT OF THE
LUCK OF TROY

*

Strong Tydeus' son should with Odysseus scale
The great wall . . . and should bear away
Pallas the Gracious, with her free consent,
Whose image was the sure defence of Troy:
Yea, for not even a god, how wrath so e'er
Had power to lay the City of Priam waste
While that immortal shape stood warder there.

QUINTUS SMYRNAEUS
Fall of Troy (Translated by A. S. Way)

CHAPTER NINE

PARIS was immensely proud of himself for shooting Achilles; and now that Hector was dead he would, of course, be the next King of Troy when Priam died.

Helen smiled wearily and sadly as she sat in her room, longing for her home in far-away Sparta; and the blood dripped from the Star-stone, dripped and vanished, dripped and vanished and left no mark.

One day a handsome youth, little more than a boy, came to see her. Through the quiet palace he was led, and reached the shaded room where Helen sat weaving at her loom.

'Lady,' he said, 'my name is Corythus, and I have a message for you alone, and for your lord, Prince Paris.'

Then Helen sent her maidens from the room, and with a smile took the scroll of bark which Corythus handed to her. Breaking the golden thread with which it was fastened, she opened and read – and her eyes went wide and the colour forsook her face.

'Your mother is called Oenone,' she said in a strangled voice, 'and she is the wife of Paris – and you are their son?'

Corythus nodded: 'My mother sent me,' he answered simply. 'It was time, she said, that I came to Troy and claimed my rightful place as eldest and only son of the heir apparent.'

Then in a flood all that she had lost came to Helen: Menelaus, her home, Hermione, the name of true and faithful wife. And all for what? For Paris, doubly a cheat and traitor, who had deceived both her and Oenone.

She uttered a little choking cry and slipped to the floor in a faint, while Corythus bent over her anxiously, pitying her grief, marvelling at her beauty.

At this moment Paris strode into the room. He gave one glance, and his mad jealousy flared up. Without a moment's pause he snatched the sword from his side and struck Corythus dead with a single blow.

Then, so fierce was his rage and jealousy, he would have slain Helen also, but he saw the scroll and, reading what Oenone had written, he realized what he had done. Then he flung himself upon the ground and wept.

Corythus was burnt on a great pyre as became his rank, and Paris mourned sincerely for him. Helen wept too; but she spoke no more to Paris, and sat alone day after day gazing out towards the Grecian tents, or weaving on her loom all the tales of sorrow that had befallen on account of her, since Paris had come and carried her away from her happy home in Sparta.

Paris suffered too, and grew more reckless, though he had seldom been much of a fighter since he brought Helen to Troy. And soon after this the

*He snatched the sword from his side and struck Corythus dead
with a single blow*

day came when Philoctetes was healed of his evil
wound and came out to battle among the Greeks,
bearing the great bow of Heracles in his hand.

Then for the last time the Trojans sallied out on
to the plain and fought the Greeks hand to hand,
with Paris cheering them on. Seeing him, Philoctetes fought his way fiercely through the thick of
his foes until he drew near to Paris who, on his side,
kept a sharp look-out. When he thought that
Philoctetes was in reasonable range, Paris set an

arrow to his bow and loosed at him. But Philoctetes dodged to one side so that another Greek took his death by it.

'Dog! Your day has come!' cried Philoctetes. 'Make haste to the land of shadows, and let there be an end to the destruction which you have caused!'

Then he drew the plaited cord to his breast, the great bow arched, the terrible point peeped out over the hand which held the curving wood. Loud sang the string as the death-hissing shaft sped on its way – and it missed not, though death was not yet, and the point did but graze the white wrist of Paris. Once again the avenger drew the bow and a barbed shaft screamed on its way, and this time buried itself in Paris's side.

Then Paris turned and fled into Troy, and night came down to cover the city and the plain. All through the hours of darkness the most skilful of the Trojan surgeons strove in vain to stop the terrible torment of the Hydra's burning blood, while Paris groaned and writhed sleeplessly. And before dawn he bade men carry him swiftly and silently out of Troy, up into the forests on Mount Ida; for he knew that in all the world only his deserted wife the nymph Oenone could cure him.

They came at last to her cave, where she sat weeping, ever weeping for her lost love and her slaughtered son.

Then Paris begged Oenone to save him. 'My lady,' he ended, 'I have sinned in my folly – but spare me! Save me from death!'

But Oenone answered in cold, dead tones: 'Go back to Helen and bid her to cure you! You slew our son, and you have killed my heart. Go quickly, you who are the cause of many a thousand deaths – not my son alone, but the sons of the women of Troy and of Greece cry out for vengeance.'

Then she turned away and sat silent, gazing into the distance.

They bore Paris away, down the steep slope towards Troy; but he was dead long before they reached the edge of the forest. So there they built a huge pyre and laid him upon it, and kindled it with fire.

But meanwhile Oenone repented of her anger, remembering only the love which had been between them, and the happy years when they dwelt together upon Ida, before the fatal coming of the three Immortals. So she gathered together her drugs and herbs, and hastened down the mountain side towards Troy. But presently she saw a glow ahead of her, and came suddenly to the pyre on which dead Paris lay.

Oenone gazed for a moment, and then with a bitter cry she sprang suddenly forward, and flung herself beside Paris, clasping him in her arms. Then the flames roared up, and the pyre fell in, and the ashes of Paris and Oenone were mingled in death.

Helen was free now; but the Trojans did not even think of sending her back to Menelaus. Indeed two brothers of Paris quarrelled as to which of them should now marry her; and when Priam gave her to Deiphobus, Helenus fled from Troy and was captured by the Greeks or gave himself up to them.

Odysseus brought him before the assembled kings, for Helenus was a prophet, and Calchas was at his wits' end to know why Troy had not yet fallen.

'I own no allegiance now to Troy,' said Helenus, 'and I will tell you of the one thing lacking. You must steal the Luck of Troy: the city can never be taken while that remains within its walls!'

'The Luck of Troy?' asked Agamemnon, puzzled.

'The Palladium,' answered Helenus, 'the stone which fell from Heaven in the days of King Ilus. It is said that Athena made it in memory of her companion Pallas, and that Zeus cast it down at the prayer of King Ilus to show where Troy should be built. But certainly no city can fall in which the Palladium rests. Of old we kept it secretly in a temple on Mount Ida – and Troy fell when Heracles came against it with Peleus and Telamon. But when Paris brought Helen to Troy, my father King Priam, by my advice, brought the Palladium to the Temple of Athena in Troy town.'

Helenus would say no more, and at length it was decided that some spy must make his way into Troy and discover how the Palladium could be stolen.

Odysseus, most cunning of the Greeks, volunteered for this service. He dressed himself in rags, got some of the Greeks to beat him until the blood ran down his face and back and covered himself in filth: there was no beggar in all the Greek camp so foul as he. In this disguise he won admission into Troy, pretending that he had been beaten and driven away by the cruel Greeks.

The Trojans welcomed him, hoping to obtain news of the Greek plans, and Odysseus played his part so well that no one suspected him, and whatever he told them was believed.

Beggar though he was, the Trojans decided that this valuable ally must be treated as well as possible. So he was taken to the house of Helen and Deiphobus to be bathed and clothed in decent clothes, and entertained.

Helen herself tended him, anxious for any news of the Greeks – and in spite of all his cunning she at length recognized him as Odysseus. For a long time he denied it with clever words, but at length Helen swore by the most solemn oaths not to betray him, and he confessed that she was right.

Then Helen wept, and told him how wretched she was. 'When Paris died,' she ended, 'the last touch of the strange magic of Aphrodite faded from me. I scarcely could remember that I had not hated him – and oh, how I hate Deiphobus who has me now!'

'Could you not escape to us?' asked Odysseus.

'Escape? I have tried again and again,' sighed Helen. 'Only the guards along the Trojan walls could tell you how often I have tried – how many times they or Deiphobus have caught me with the rope already round my waist – once I was actually hanging down outside the wall . . . But how would I be received in the Greek camp I who, alas, am the cause of so much misery? And my husband, Menelaus, surely he hates me – though it was not of my own free will that I went with Paris in that night of evil magic so many weary years ago.'

After this they spoke long together, making plans for the theft of the Palladium, and for the taking of Troy. But Odysseus the over-cunning did not tell Helen everything; though in his mind he was already inventing the device of the Wooden Horse, he spoke of it to her only in double meanings and half-concealed hints, and left her doubting and even rather resentful.

But that night she helped him to escape from Troy, allowing the watchmen to catch her in one of her own attempts and so distracting their attention while Odysseus climbed down to Diomedes who was waiting for him. But she herself remained in Troy to do her part on the night of the great attack.

Before this could be launched, however, the Palladium had still to be stolen, and on a dark night Odysseus and Diomedes came for it. They entered Troy this time by means of a narrow, evil-smelling drain arched with great stones – a drain that may be seen at Troy to this day. This low tunnel led them, through mire and filth, to the very middle of Troy. It came up near the temple and here Theano the priestess, wife of Antenor, gave up the image to them, and they were able to carry it away – though not to enter the city again by that path.

Outside in the pale moon-light the evil magic in the misshapen idol began to exert itself upon the thieves. For as Diomedes walked ahead with it on his back a madness came upon Odysseus: not knowing what he was doing, he fell behind his friend, drew his sword and crept stealthily up, meaning to stab him in the back. But as luck would have it the moon shone out from behind a cloud as he was about to strike, and the flash of light on the sword-blade caught the eye of Diomedes who wheeled round just in time to avoid the blow. The madness was succeeded by a blank horror: Odysseus dropped his weapon and allowed Diomedes to drive him in front of him like a cow while he beat him with the flat of his sword.

When they came to their senses neither Odysseus nor Diomedes bore any malice towards each other. But the Greeks decided that the Luck of Troy would bring only bad luck to them, and carried it hastily to a shrine of Athena on Mount Ida. There it remained until after the Fall of Troy, when Aeneas took it with him on his wanderings.

Whether or not the loss of the Palladium made any difference to Troy, it was immediately after its theft that Odysseus suggested the plan of the Wooden Horse. He went off to Mount Ida with Epeius the skilled ship-wright and a band of men to fell trees, and brought back the timber to the Greek camp. Here a high wall was built to hide from the Trojans what was going on, and Epeius set to work, using all his skill to build the Horse according to the plans prepared by Odysseus.

First he made the hollow body of the horse, in size like a curved ship; and he fitted a neck to the front of it with a purple fringed mane sprinkled with gold. The mane fell below the cunningly fashioned head which had eyes of blood-red amethyst surrounded with gems of sea-green beryl. In the mouth he set rows of jagged white teeth, and a golden bit with a jewelled bridle. And he made secret air-holes in the nostrils and the wide mouth and the high-pricked ears.

Then he fitted legs to the Horse, and a flowing tail twisted with gold and hung with tassels. The hooves were shod with bronze and mounted with polished tortoise-shell, and under them were set wheels so that the Horse might move easily over the ground.

Under the Horse there was a secret trap-door so cunningly hidden that no one, looking at the Horse from outside, could suspect it; and the door fastened from within with a special catch that only Epeius could undo.

So high and so wide was the Horse that it could not pass through any gate of Troy, and the secret hollow inside it was big enough for thirty men to enter and lie concealed with all their armour and weapons.

When all was ready, Odysseus begged Agamemnon to summon all the Kings and Princes of the Greek force, and he rose up in the assembly and said:

'My friends, now is the secret ambush prepared
– thanks be to Athena my Immortal counsellor
and protector. Let us set all upon the hazard of a
single exploit – an exploit that will live for ever on
the lips of men. Let those of you who dare follow
me into the Horse: for my plans are all laid, and
my cousin Sinon is instructed how to beguile the
Trojans. You, my lord Agamemnon, when we are
safely in the Horse, must wait until darkness, then
pull down the wall surrounding it and destroy the
camp. Afterwards sail away with all our ships –
but wait in hiding beyond the island of Tenedos.
On the following night, if all is well, Sinon will
kindle a fire on the Grave of Achilles as a signal.
Come all of you then back to land, and in darkness
and silence speed to Troy town and lay it low!
For the gates will be open – and Helen will set a
lamp in her window to guide you.'

Then all the Greeks cried out in praise of Odysseus and the greatness of his scheme – and all
wished to accompany him into the Horse. But
besides himself and Epeius he chose out no more
than twenty-eight, and these included Menelaus
and Teucer the brother of dead Ajax, Aias the son
of Oileus, Thrasymedes the son of Nestor, Eumelus
the son of Admetus and two sons of Theseus
called Demophon and Acamas who had come to
Troy with Menestheus the King of Athens to
rescue their grandmother Aethra who was still
Helen's attendant.

The thirty climbed up the ladder into the Horse,
drew it after them and closed the door, which

Epeius then sat upon, while Odysseus settled himself in the Horse's neck to look out through the hidden holes.

Then Agamemnon caused the walls to be levelled, the camp to be torn down and the whole army embarked in the ships.

When day dawned the plain of Troy lay empty and deserted except for the great Horse towering there alone. And on the wide sea not a ship was to be seen.

CHAPTER 10

THE WOODEN HORSE

*

But Helen stood bright-eyed as glancing day
Nearby the Horse, and with a straying hand
Did stroke it here and there, and listening stand,
Leaning her head towards its gilded flank,
And strain to hear men's breath behind the plank.

MAURICE HEWLETT
Helen Redeemed

Morning dawned over the windy plain of Troy, and the Trojans looked out towards the great camp of the Greeks which had stood there so long – looked, and rubbed their eyes and looked again.

The camp was a deserted ruin of tumbled stone, and charred huts and palisades; and there were no ships to be seen drawn up on the shore, nor upon the sea.

While they were wondering at this and hardly able to believe their eyes, scouts came hastening to King Priam.

'The Greeks have indeed gone!' they cried. 'The camp lies in ashes; there is not a man, not a ship to be seen. But there stands in the midst of the ruins a great Wooden Horse the like of which we have never seen.'

Then the gates of Troy were flung open and out poured young and old, laughing and shouting in their joy that the Greeks were gone at last. Priam led the way with Queen Hecuba and their only surviving son Polites and their daughters Cassandra and Polyxena; and they came to the ruins and stood gazing at the great Wooden Horse.

And now they could see letters of gold inscribed on the Horse's side:

ΤΗΣ ΕΙΣ ΟΙΚΟΝ ΑΝΑΚΟΜΙΔΗΣ
ΕΛΛΗΝΕΣ ΑΘΗΝΑ ΧΑΡΙΣΤΗΡΙΟΝ

(*For their return home, the Greeks dedicate this thank-offering to Athena*).

'But there stands in the midst of the ruins a great Wooden Horse the like of which we have never seen.'

At once a great argument broke out among the Trojans as to what should be done with the Horse.

'It is a gift to Athena,' cried one chief, 'so let us take it into Troy and place it in her temple!'

'No, no!' cried another, 'rather let us fling it into the sea!'

The arguments grew fierce: many wished to destroy it, but more to keep it as a memorial of the war – and Priam favoured this course.

Then Laocoon the priest, a man of violent temper who had already insulted Poseidon the Immortal Lord of the Sea by failing to offer him his due sacrifices, rushed up crying:

'Wretched men, are you mad? Do you not realize that the *Greeks* have made this? May it not be some cunning engine devised by that evil creature Odysseus to break down our walls or spy into our houses. There is something guileful about it, I am certain, and I warn you, Trojans, not to trust this Horse. Whatever it is, I fear the Greeks most when they make us gifts!'

So saying Laocoon hurled his spear at the Horse, and there came from it a strange clash and clang as of metal.

Then indeed the Trojans might have grown suspicious, and broken open the Horse with axes as some suggested; but at that moment several shepherds appeared, leading between them the wretched figure of a man who was caked from head to foot with mud and filth and dried blood; and his hands were fastened together with fetters of bronze.

'Great King of Troy!' he gasped. 'Save me! Pity me! I am a Greek, I confess it, but no man among you can hate the Greeks as I do – and it is within my power to make Troy safe for ever.'

'Speak,' said Priam briefly. 'Who are you, and what can you tell us?'

'My name is Sinon,' was the answer, 'and I am a cousin of Odysseus – of that most hateful and fiendish among men. Listen to what chanced. You have all heard of Palamedes? He was a Greek, and your enemy, but his gifts to mankind, and his wondrous inventions benefit you and all men. Odysseus hated him, for he it was who saw through his feigned madness and forced him to come to the war. At length that hatred could be endured no longer, and Odysseus of the many wiles devised a hideous plot whereby Palamedes was accused of betraying the Greek army to you Trojans. On the evidence of a forged letter he was convicted and stoned to death – and I alone knew that Odysseus wrote the letter and arranged the plot. Alas, I reproached my cousin with what he had done, and ever after he sought to have me slain.

'At length the time came when the Greeks despaired of conquering Troy: for it was revealed that never could they do so during this invasion. But our Immortal Lady Athena made it known to us that if we returned to Greece and set out afresh, we should conquer Troy. But first we must make this monstrous Horse as an offering to her – and make it so large that it could never be drawn into

Troy: for *whatever city contains this Horse can never be conquered.*

'So the Horse was made. But Odysseus beguiled Calchas the prophet into declaring that, even as the Greek forces could not leave Aulis until the innocent maiden Iphigenia was sacrificed, so they could not leave Troy without the sacrifice of a noble warrior: and, by the evil workings of Odysseus, I was chosen as the victim.

'Last night they would have sacrificed me: but rendered desperate I broke away, and fled to hide myself in the foul mud of a noisome marsh that drains all Troy. Then the wind rose suddenly and the Greeks sailed away; but whether another was sacrificed instead of me, I cannot say. Only this I can tell you, noble Priam: this Horse is sacred to Athena and – since they have treated me so cruelly I can betray their secrets without incurring the anger of the Immortals – if you take it into Troy, the Greeks will never conquer you. Instead, you will be sailing to Greece, to sack rich Mycenae and proud Athens, Argos of the many horses and windy Iolcus and Sparta in the fertile plain of hollow Lacedaemon.'

Then Priam and the other Trojan lords consulted together, and many of them were minded to believe Sinon; but others still doubted. While fate hung in the balance, there came two serpents out of the sea and made for the altar where Laocoon had retired with his two sons to offer up a sacrifice to the Sealord Poseidon. Straight to the place they went, terrible to be seen, and seized upon the two boys, and began to crush them in their deadly coils.

Laocoon strove to save his sons; but the serpents seized him too, and in a little while all three lay dead beside the altar of Poseidon.

Now all the Trojans cried out that Laocoon had been justly rewarded by the angry Immortals for casting his spear at the glorious offering made to Athena. Without further ado they twined the Horse about with garlands of flowers, and dragged it across the plain towards the city.

When they reached the gate, the Horse proved too big to enter by it: but the Trojans gaily pulled down a section of the wall, and brought it through in triumph, right to the courtyard of Athena's temple from which the Palladium, the Luck of Troy, had been stolen.

As evening fell, Cassandra came and stood beside the Horse:

'Cry, Trojans, cry!' she screamed. 'Your doom is upon you! I see warriors come from their hollow abode! I see Troy burning, her sons slaughtered and her daughters carried away to slavery! Cry, Trojans, cry! For madness has come upon you, and your doom is here!'

But no one would believe her, for still the curse was upon her that she must speak the truth and not be believed; and presently she went into the temple of Athena and knelt in prayer before a statue of the Immortal whom she worshipped.

Night fell, and the Trojans feasted and revelled in their joy that the Great War was over and the

Greeks had gone. At last worn out with excitement and celebration, they fell asleep, leaving few guards by the walls and gates – and few indeed that were sober.

But Aphrodite was loath to admit that Paris's people were about to be destroyed on account of the bribe which she had given him for the Golden Apple; and she made one last attempt to save the Trojans.

She went to Helen as she sat waiting in the palace, and cast her spell over her once more – though it was but faint and very brief. But Helen forgot for an hour that she hated Deiphobus, forgot that she was longing with all her heart for Menelaus and her lost Hermione. She rose like one in a dream and went to seek for the Trojan husband whom she detested.

'Dear my lord,' she said in her sweet voice as she laid her hand on his arm. 'Come with me, I beg you: for I would see this wondrous Horse made by the Greeks who were once my people.'

Intoxicated with joy at this sudden change in Helen's manner towards him, Deiphobus went with her willingly, and they came together into the courtyard of Athena's temple.

'Suppose,' mused Helen in a dreamy voice, 'the Kings of Greece – Menelaus, and Agamemnon, Odysseus and Diomedes and the rest – suppose they were all shut up inside this Horse!'

'If you think that,' exclaimed Deiphobus, 'we must have it broken open at once!'

'No,' murmured Helen, 'I have a better means

than that. If they are there, I will lure them out!'

Now all her life Helen had the power of mimicry: she could assume any voice so perfectly that no one who heard could tell her from the actual person.

So now, walking round and round the Horse, she called softly and sweetly, first in her own voice:

'Menelaus! Menelaus! Come to me, my lord and my love!' And then she called to Agamemnon in the voice of her sister Clytemnestra; and to Odysseus in the voice of her cousin Penelope. To Diomedes she called in the very tones of his wife Aegialia; and to each in the tones of one dearest to him.

Inside the Horse the heroes were sitting trembling and alert: only Neoptolemus showed no fear but gazed fiercely in front of him and gripped his sword. But when they heard their wives calling to them, the voices they had not heard for ten long, wretched years, the tears coursed down their cheeks and they found it hard indeed to stop themselves from answering.

Only Anticlus, the youngest man in the Horse, could not bear it. When he heard his wife Laodamia calling to him, he leapt forward to unfasten the trapdoor and he opened his mouth to answer her. But watchful Odysseus caught hold of him in time, gripping him tightly and placing a hand firmly over his mouth.

But Anticlus seemed mad with his desire to cry

out and escape from the Horse, and in deadly
terror lest he should utter a sound and they should
all perish, Odysseus held him tighter and tighter;
and, without meaning it, he choked him so that

*All that night she sat in her window with a bright lamp
beside her*

Anticlus died there in the Horse, and his friends
wept silently for him and wrapped his body in a
cloak.

'There is no one in the Horse,' exclaimed Deiphobus at length. 'Come to bed, Helen, I am weary
and would sleep.'

So they went together to Helen's bed-chamber in a high tower overlooking the plain of Troy, and Deiphobus slept – for the last time. When he was asleep, the spell of Aphrodite passed from Helen, and she was overcome with shame and self-loathing at what she had done. All that night she sat in her window with a bright lamp beside her so that the Greeks could find Troy in the darkness, and she held out her white arms as if to draw Menelaus to her. And ever the Star-stone on her breast dripped its red drops which fell on to her snowy raiment, fell and vanished – fell and vanished – and left no stain.

Behind her a great silence lay upon the doomed city of Troy. Not a sound of song or of revelry broke the stillness of the night, not even the baying of a dog was to be heard, but perfect silence reigned as if Night held her breath, awaiting the sudden outbreak of the noise of war and death.

Through that silence the Greek fleet stole back to the beaches; for on the mound which marked Achilles's tomb a great fire burned, kindled by Sinon. And from Helen's window the light shone out so that the Greeks drew nearer and nearer to Troy, silent and sure, stealing through the early night to be there before the moon rose.

And when the first silvery beams came stealing over the black shape of distant Ida, Odysseus gave the word, and Epeius undid the bolt and opened the door beneath the belly of the Wooden Horse. In his eager haste Echion sprang out before the ladder was ready, and the fall killed him. But the other heroes climbed down in safety, stole through the silent streets, killed what sleepy sentinels there were on watch and opened the gates of Troy to Agamemnon and the armies of Greece.

CHAPTER II

THE FALL OF TROY

*

Come, Helen, come, give me my soul again:
Here will I dwell, for Heaven is in those lips,
And all is dross that is not Helena . . .
Oh thou art fairer than the evening air
Clad in the beauty of a thousand stars.

MARLOWE
Dr Faustus

CHAPTER ELEVEN

THE storm of war broke without warning over the doomed city of Troy. Suddenly the Greeks were everywhere, killing the Trojans in their sleep, killing them half awake, killing them in little bands – those few who had time to seize their weapons.

Old men, women, children died on that terrible night, for the ten-year-old fury of the Greeks made them merciless during those hours of darkness.

Priam met his end at the threshold of his own palace. When the alarm broke out he would have buckled on his armour and gone out to fight, but Hecuba persuaded him to remain with her by the altar of Zeus in the courtyard of the palace.

But presently their son Polites came staggering into the yard, wounded and pursued by Neoptolemus who was mad with the lust of slaughter. Right in front of his parents' eyes he struck the unfortunate boy through the body with his spear so that he fell dead on the altar steps before them.

Then Old Priam sprang to his feet.

'Ah what wickedness!' he cried. 'Thus to kill my son before my face! That Achilles would never have done; he was merciful! He gave me the body of Hector when I went to beg it, and treated me kindly, remembering his own father. Surely you are no true son of his!'

So saying, Priam flung a spear at Neoptolemus; but the arm of the old king had lost its strength, and the weapon clattered harmlessly down on to the stone floor.

'Indeed,' laughed Neoptolemus grimly. 'If you find me so much worse than my father you had better hasten down to the realm of the dead and tell him about me!'

With that he seized Priam by the hair, dragged him to the door of the palace and cut off his head.

But all kindness was not forgotten that night. Odysseus saw one of the sons of Antenor attacked by two Greeks, and protected him and helped him home to his house. For he remembered how Antenor had entertained him and Menelaus when they came to Troy to demand the surrender of Helen, and how it was Antenor who had saved their lives when treacherous Paris tried to urge the Trojans to murder them.

So now he hung a leopard skin from the window of the house as a sign that no one in it was to be hurt; and in the morning he saw to it that Antenor and his wife Theano, who had handed over the Palladium, were allowed to escape with their children and servants, and an ass laden with the choicest of their possessions.

Another Trojan prince who was allowed to escape was the pious Aeneas. King Agamemnon saw him walking through the streets with his old father Anchises on his shoulders carrying the holy images from his house, and leading by the hand his little son Ascanius, while Creusa his wife followed behind. Pleased to see such family affection, Agamemnon gave orders that they were to be spared, and Aeneas won safely to the slopes of Ida with his precious burden, and his beloved child. But Creusa was lost in the turmoil as they left the city, and he never found her again.

The two sons of Theseus, Acamas and Demophon, struck no blow save when a Trojan attacked them. But they searched through Troy for their grandmother Aethra who had been a slave attending on Helen ever since Castor and Polydeuces took Aphidna and rescued their sister after Theseus had carried her away as a child. When they found Aethra, still beautiful and regal, though so very ancient, they led her, with all the honour due to a queen, out of Troy and down to their tall ships; and they claimed no other spoils or rewards for their services in the war.

While these things were happening, Menelaus was seeking through Troy for Helen, and at length Odysseus guided him to the house of Deiphobus. There Menelaus entered sword in hand and a fury of jealousy in his heart; but Odysseus remained at the door and fought his fiercest and most desperate battle of any in the whole war.

Up to Helen's chamber went Menelaus, and there Deiphobus met him, heavy with drink and sleep. They fought across the bed, and before long Menelaus struck the sword out of the prince's hand and had him at his mercy.

'Dog!' he hissed. 'Never again shall you see the dawn over Troy town, for justice comes at last, however slow her steps, and no man may elude great Themis. Now black death has trapped you, here in my wife's bower – and I would that I could have dealt out the same punishment to Paris!'

Then he plunged his sword into the evil heart of Deiphobus so that he fell and died there upon the bed, and his wicked spirit fled to the judgement hall of Hades.

But Helen came to Menelaus out of the shadows and knelt to him, love struggling with fear in her wonderful eyes as she looked up at him.

Then Menelaus raised his bloodstained sword, and a terrible urge went through him as he thought of all that he had suffered for this woman's sake, and all the woes she had brought upon Greece and Troy.

Yet in a moment the sword fell useless from his hand, and as he gazed upon that beauty which surpassed the beauty of all other women, the rage and jealousy went out of his heart. She knelt before him, the magic Star-stone rising and falling on her white breast, while the red drips fell and vanished – fell and vanished – and left no stain. And suddenly, he knew that there was no stain on her either, and that their love had been only interrupted by the spells of Aphrodite – but not broken.

'Helen!' he said, and in another moment he held the World's Desire in his arms, and the bitterness of the long years fell away from them and was forgotten.

Cold morning dawned over the stricken city, and still the Greeks slew and slew until the streets and houses were heaped with dead. And without the city the captive women were herded together in weeping droves among the piles of loot. Cruel Neoptolemus took Andromache as his prize, and flung Astyanax, Hector's baby son, to his death from the walls of Troy.

But she clung to the statue of Athena and begged him to spare her

'He is a fool who kills the father and lets the children live,' was his brutal excuse. 'If the boy had grown to be a man he might have sought to slay me, since my father slew his. And we want no more kings of Troy!'

Aias the wild son of Oileus tried to grab Cassandra as his share of the more noble captives, but she clung to the statue of Athena and begged him to spare her, since she was sworn to the service of the gods of Olympus. Aias however shouted that he feared neither god nor man, and dragged her roughly away.

Then the whole temple was shaken with an earthquake, and the very statue turned up its eyes in horror. And when Agamemnon heard of this, he had Aias chased out of the Greek camp with threats of execution, since his deed might call down the vengeance of Athena on them all. Agamemnon, however, felt that as the deed had been done, it was a pity to lose so lovely and high-born a captive, and he took Cassandra himself to be his handmaiden.

But Aias sailed away in a fury, cursing Agamemnon and defying all the Immortals, and Athena in particular. But Poseidon wrecked his ship in a great storm and he was cast up on a rock in the middle of the sea where he drew himself into safety above the raging waves. This was his last chance, but still his pride was unbroken, and he taunted the Immortals, crying:

'You are not gods, why you cannot even drown the man who has insulted you!'

The lightning flashed ominously through the storm clouds, but in his madness Aias cried again:

'You think to frighten me with your thunder, do you? Lightning, I defy you!' At this Zeus took the matter into his own hands and hurled a thunderbolt which split the rock and sent Aias to his doom on the instant.

When Troy had been thoroughly pillaged, and the captives taken down to the sea-shore, the Greeks set fire to the town. Then the tall towers burned, and the houses were reduced to ashes. The falling buildings brought the walls crashing down with them, and the Greeks completed the destruction so that only the foundations remained over which the weeds grew and the earth was piled up, until three thousand years later the remains were uncovered, and today stand gaunt and mysterious above the plain to bear witness to the basic truth which blind Homer wove into the first and greatest of romantic tales.

The Greeks went down to their ships and remained for a while encamped near the Tomb of Achilles at the mouth of the River Scamander; some even crossed the Hellespont to the utmost tip of Europe: for the winds blew strongly across the Aegean Sea, and there was no sailing west or south.

When Menelaus led Helen down to the ships, the soldiers cried out that she must be slain, and took up stones to cast at her. But when they beheld her beauty, the stones fell from their hands, and they stood in awe as if she had been an Immortal, nor had they any further wish to do her aught but honour.

Day after day the winds were contrary, until Calchas declared that, just as when they left Aulis, there must be a sacrifice of a royal maiden.

That same night Neoptolemus dreamt that his father Achilles rose from the tomb, shaking his terrible spear and crying:

'Shame on you, Greeks! All have your reward from the spoils of captured Troy, save only I! Give to me the prize which by right is mine, even the fairest of Royal Maidens – Polyxena, daughter of Priam. If I have her not, never will you come in safety to fair Hellas!'

When Neoptolemus told of his dream, all doubt was at an end. The soldiers cried aloud for the sacrifice: Polyxena, they remembered, was loved by Achilles in his life-time, for he had seen her when she leant from the walls of Troy to fling her bracelets into the scale at the ransoming of Hector's body. It was even said that there had been a secret marriage – of which the Trojans took advantage by adding that Achilles had offered to betray the Greeks if Priam gave him Polyxena.

Certainly it was believed that Achilles demanded Polyxena to be his bride in the Elysian Fields, and Neoptolemus slew her on his father's tomb, despite the piteous prayers of her wretched mother, Queen Hecuba.

The aged queen of Troy was released from captivity after her daughter's death, and given to her son Helenus, who carried her away shrieking curses on the Greeks. The story got about that as soon as he landed with her beyond the Hellespont, Hecuba turned into a black hound – just such a hound as howls at night among the graves, or follows in the train of Hecate the Queen of Witches.

Besides Helenus, the Greeks allowed Antenor to sail away with all his family, servants and possessions. This honest Trojan made his way to the head of the Adriatic Sea and founded a new Troy, which in later days was called Venice. A son of his travelled to the land which was afterwards known as France, and the French royal family could trace their descent from him.

The few other Trojans who escaped from the destruction of Troy fled on to Mount Ida and joined Aeneas who was in hiding there. When the Greeks had sailed – which they were able to do soon after Polyxena had been sacrificed – Aeneas and his companions cut down trees, built great ships and sailed away to seek for a new home.

Early in their wanderings they came to an island on which grazed some fine fat cattle, and there was no sign of any herdsmen. So they killed several, cooked them and settled down for a good meal. But no sooner had they begun to eat than the Harpies – the same winged women with sharp claws that the Argonauts had met and Zetes and Calais had driven away from the land of King Phineus – swooped down and snatched their meat away. Three times they tried to eat, and three times the Harpies robbed them: and after the third time one of the Harpies perched on a rock and cried:

'You Trojans who kill our cattle and try to drive us from our own island, listen to me! Sail away quickly, and doubtless you will reach the new home which Aphrodite is planning for you in a land called Italy: but I tell you that before you build the walls of your new city, you will be so hungry that you will be driven to eat the very tables on which you place your food!'

After this the Trojan fleet set sail sorrowfully, and met with several adventures during their wanderings. Old Anchises died, and was buried in Sicily; and then Hera stirred up the winds so that several of the ships were wrecked, and the rest of them were driven to North Africa where they were made welcome in the newly built city of Carthage, where the Phoenician called Elissa by the Greeks and Dido by the Trojans, was Queen.

She and her Phoenicians had sailed away from the coast of Asia far to the south of Troy some years earlier, and landed in North Africa where they demanded a site on which to build a city. The king of that country did not want them, but he said: 'You may have just as much land as the hide of an ox will enclose!'

Dido however took an ox-hide and cut it into such thin strips that it surrounded all the the lands she needed – and Carthage was built on that site.

After resting there for some time, Aeneas was anxious to sail on his way, but Dido had fallen in love with him and wished him to marry her and become King of Carthage.

Aeneas, however, stole away by night with all his ships: and when Dido found that he had cheated and deserted her, she killed herself. But Aeneas sailed happily on his way, and at last came to Italy at a place called Cumae where dwelt a famous prophetess called the Sibyl. She told him that he was near the spot where he must build his city, and that this city would in years to come rule the world and be called Rome.

On went Aeneas rejoicing, and came presently to a great river with yellow water, which was called the Tiber. Up this he sailed, and anchored at last in a beautiful wood.

Here they landed and collected fruits to eat. As they had lost all their dishes during the voyage, they mixed flour and water and made plates and tables of dough. When the fruits were done and they were still hungry, they began to eat the dough, and the boy Ascanius exclaimed laughing:

'What, are we so hungry that we even eat our tables!'

Then Aeneas knew that they had reached the place where his new city was to be. He had many adventures before it was built, but all ended well, and he married Lavinia the only daughter of King Latinus who ruled that country.

Their descendants became Kings of Rome, and in later years Emperors of the Roman Empire. One grandson of Aeneas called Brutus was said to have wandered away to the island of Albion in the North-west, and become king of it: that island was re-named after him and has ever since been known as Britain, and its kings and queens are said to be descended from him.

But Troy itself was never again a great city.

Several small towns were built on the spot in after years, but were all soon destroyed and quickly forgotten: its glory departed from it three thousand years ago – to live for ever in song and story, and to stir our imaginations even to this day.

CHAPTER 12

AGAMEMNON AND HIS CHILDREN

*

Not yet to dark Cassandra lying low
   In rich Mycenae do the fates relent;
The bones of Agamemnon are a show,
   And ruined is his royal monument.

ANDREW LANG
Sonnet on the Iliad

CHAPTER TWELVE

AFTER the sacrifice of Polyxena the wind fell and the Greeks were able to sail away; but their adventures were by no means ended: Diomedes, Nestor and Agamemnon were the only leaders who came straight home – and of these only Nestor found all well with his kingdom and was able to settle down comfortably to enjoy his old age in peace.

Diomedes suffered ship-wreck on the way, but it did not delay him for long. However, when he reached Argos he found that his wife had married someone else, and that the people were quite content with their new ruler and not in the least pleased to see him and his companions back again. In disgust he sailed off once more; and finally he came to Italy, settled there and lived to a ripe old age, much honoured by his new countrymen.

Agamemnon was not so fortunate. Ever since the sacrifice of Iphigenia at Aulis, Clytemnestra's hatred of him had grown more and more bitter. Finally she decided that he had forfeited all right to be her husband, and she married his cousin Aegisthus instead.

She did not let Agamemnon know this, however, and she kept a watchman on the roof of the palace of Mycenae to watch for the signal that Troy had fallen, which was to be brought by a series of beacon fires on the tops of lofty mountains.

When the news came of the sack of Troy, she

made haste to send young Orestes away to his uncle King Strophius, and she kept Agamemnon's two daughters Electra and Chrysothemis well out of the way. As for Aegisthus, he remained hidden in the palace while Clytemnestra went out to welcome Agamemnon as if really delighted to have him home again.

Agamemnon came up to the palace in great pride and triumph, and entered over a purple carpet as became the Conqueror of Troy. With him he brought much treasure and many Trojan captives of whom the chief was Cassandra, the dark, mysterious daughter of King Priam who could foresee the future but whose prophecies were never believed.

Now she stood on the wide terrace, high above the great plain of Argos, and cried aloud that death waited in the palace – death for Agamemnon and death for herself.

Then, with head held high, she went in to her doom, noble and fearless as befitted a Princess of Troy – and there cruel Clytemnestra slew her.

But first the Queen of Mycenae, still pretending to welcome Agamemnon, led him to the marble-floored bathroom, and bathed him with her own hands, bidding him make haste to the feast which waited them.

Still swelling with pride at this royal welcome after his mighty deeds, Agamemnon rose from his bath, and took the finely embroidered shirt which Clytemnestra had made for him. She slipped it over his head, and the folds of it fell about him, and he was caught in it: for she had sewn up the neck and sleeves.

While he struggled in this silken web, she struck him down with an axe; and Aegisthus came out of

While he struggled in this silken web, she struck him down with an axe

his hiding place and helped in the slaying of the King of Men. And when Agamemnon lay dead, Clytemnestra took up her axe once more and went to meet and slay Cassandra: for in spite of her hatred of Agamemnon, she was still jealous.

After Agamemnon was dead and buried, Clytemnestra and Aegisthus ruled Mycenae. He wished to have Orestes killed, but Clytemnestra was not quite so wicked as that, and she refused to say where the young prince was hidden. Her younger daughter, Chrysothemis, did not seem to mind what had happened; but the elder, Electra, hated Aegisthus and could not forgive her mother. Clytemnestra would not consent to her death either, but fearing lest she should marry a prince and persuade him to punish her and Aegisthus she gave Electra to a poor peasant who lived in a cottage not far from the city of Mycenae.

This good man, however, felt that marriage with him would be an insult to the daughter of so great a king.

'Princess,' he said to Electra. 'Let us pretend to have obeyed the wicked commands of Queen Clytemnestra: but it need only be a pretence marriage – then when some brave Prince comes along, to help you, you will be able to marry him.'

So matters stood for seven years. Aegisthus reigned in Mycenae, though very much under the powerful thumb of Clytemnestra, and boasted often that he feared no vengeance; but in fact he was in constant terror lest Orestes should return and slay him. Electra desired above all things that this should happen; and whenever she could do so in safety sent messages to her brother reminding him that vengeance was still to be accomplished.

Orestes grew up at his uncle's court, and his dearest friend Pylades, the son of King Strophius, swore to stand by him in whatever he might do.

At last Aegisthus grew so angry with Electra for her constant threats and taunts that he declared he would send her to a distant city and shut her up in a deep dungeon. Then she sent in haste to Orestes, and he knew that the time had come to act.

First of all he visited Delphi to consult the oracle of Apollo: for he was in a great dilemma. According to Greek beliefs it was his duty to avenge his father's murder by killing the murderers; this was all right so far as Aegisthus was concerned – but to kill his mother was the worst of all crimes, and he knew that if he committed it, the Furies would pursue him and drive him mad.

Nevertheless Apollo, speaking through the mouth of his priestess at Delphi, commanded him to proceed and fear nothing, for though suffering would follow, all should be well in the end.

Consequently Orestes set off in disguise, accompanied by Pylades, and arrived at Mycenae where Electra was overjoyed to see them.

'Let Pylades go to the palace with the news that Orestes is dead,' suggested Electra, 'then Aegisthus will be off his guard and you will soon find a chance to kill him. As for our mother, I will send word that I am ill, and she will certainly come and visit me: all you have to do then is to lie in wait here at the cottage.'

All worked out just as they had planned. Both Orestes and Pylades went to tell the false news to Aegisthus, who was so pleased that he invited them to help him offer a great sacrifice of gratitude to the Immortals. And at the sacrifice Orestes slew him, and revealing who he was, won instant forgiveness from the people of Mycenae, who were thankful to be rid of the tyrant and have the son of Agamemnon as their king.

But when Orestes, urged on to the deed by Electra, killed Clytemnestra also, the Mycenaeans were not so anxious to have him. Indeed they were prepared to stone him to death: but before they could do so, madness fell upon him and the Furies came up from the realm of Hades to haunt him, and to pursue him wherever he might go until at length he should die.

While matters were still in doubt, old King Tyndareus of Sparta, Clytemnestra's father, arrived at Mycenae, bringing with him his granddaughter Hermione who had been promised in marriage to Orestes. Tyndareus came because news had reached him that Menelaus and Helen, after long wanderings, had been sighted off Cape Malea. But when he learned what Orestes had done, he urged the people of Mycenae to stone him and Electra without further delay.

In desperation Electra captured Hermione, brought her on to the roof of the palace and when the people arrived with Tyndareus at their head she cried:

'I have the Princess of Sparta here, and I will kill her before your eyes unless you let Orestes go free!'

At this crucial moment Immortal Apollo appeared to them, and told the people of Mycenae that Orestes had done the deed by his command.

'He must wander as an exile for one year,' Apollo concluded, 'and at the end of that time come to Athens for judgement. But when all is ended, he will return here to be your king, and he shall marry Hermione.'

All happened as Apollo directed. Orestes set out on his wanderings, pursued by the Furies and accompanied by his faithful Pylades. He visited many places during his year of exile, but could never stay anywhere for long, since always the Furies would overtake him and drive him onward, ever onward.

When the year was over, Orestes came to Athens, and there the great court of the Areopagus met on the Hill of Ares to try his case. Erigone, daughter of Aegisthus and Clytemnestra, hastened from Mycenae to plead for the punishment of Orestes, but nevertheless the twelve judges were equally divided. Then Athena, the Immortal Lady of Athens, appeared on the Hill of Ares and spoke to the Areopagus:

'You just and mighty men of Athens, hear my decree! Long may this Court remain, and ever shall it be famous for the justice and righteousness of its judgements. And when, as now, the judgement falls equally on two sides, the casting vote shall rest with me: and my vote shall be the vote of mercy. Orestes goes free, pardoned and acquitted: and so shall all after him who stand before this Court and find equal judgement!'

So Orestes went forth, cleared of the blood-guilt and free of the Furies. But they, filled with anger, demanded of Athena whether they were to be dishonoured and deprived of their rights.

'On the contrary,' answered the wise Immortal, 'your honour shall be made all the greater by this day's judgement. Beneath the rock of Ares' Hill shall be your shrine, and there all honour shall be done to the three of you, Alecto, Megaera and Tisiphone. You will preside over Justice, seeing that evil is punished: but no longer will you be called the Furies – I change your name to the Eumenides, the "Kindly Powers", for it is more noble to cherish the right than to punish the wrong.'

All was at peace now; but Orestes could not yet return to Mycenae. He had still one quest to perform before the madness and the stain could quite be washed from him. By the command of Apollo he must journey to the land of Tauris and fetch back the image of Artemis.

Tauris was at the north of the Black Sea, being the land which we now call the Crimea: and its inhabitants sacrificed all strangers who came there to their cruel idol, and flung their bodies into a fiery pit through which the flames came up from Tartarus.

Orestes and Pylades set out on their voyage in a swift ship with fifty oarsmen. They reached Tauris by night, left the ship ready in a secret cove and started inland by themselves hoping to find the image unguarded and to carry it off before morning. But a band of shepherds surprised them on their way, captured them and led them before Thoas, the savage king of the Taurians. He was delighted at having two Greek victims, and handed them straight over to the virgin priestess of Artemis with instructions to prepare them for sacrifice.

The priestess looked at the two victims pityingly, and when they were alone asked them if they were Greeks. When she learnt that they were, she spoke to them in their own language, saying that she was held there by force, being a Greek herself, and loathed the rites of human sacrifice.

'I will save one of you,' she said, 'if he will promise on his return to Greece to carry a message for me.'

'What is it?' asked Pylades. 'I will surely carry it!'

'The message,' answered the priestess, 'is to Orestes, the son of King Agamemnon. Say that his sister whom men thought was slain at Aulis, lives in this terrible place and begs of him to come with a great fleet and save her. Say that I am indeed Iphigenia!'

As seriously as possible Pylades repeated this message to Orestes himself, and then turning with a smile, said:

'Lady I have performed your request. Let Orestes himself answer it!' Then there was great rejoicing and delight as Iphigenia told Orestes how she had been carried away in a cloud from Aulis while Artemis placed a doe on the altar in her place just as Agamemnon's sword was falling.

Orestes told why he had come to Tauris, and Iphigenia nodded.

'I knew,' she said, 'that someone would come. Artemis does not like her sacred image to be drenched in blood by these barbarians: it must be brought to Greece and set in a safe place.'

Reaching up, she lifted down the image which, like the Palladium, had fallen from the sky as a meteor falls. Even as she did so, King Thoas strode into the shrine.

'Why are you so long?' he demanded. 'And why do you lift down the holy image of Artemis?'

'Alas,' exclaimed Iphigenia readily, 'as I strove to make the victims ready for the sacrifice, the image averted its eyes. Then Artemis spoke to me and said that already her shrine was polluted, since one of these men has murdered his mother, and the other is his helper. So now I must take them and the image to the shore and wash them in the salt sea. And you must bring fire and water to cleanse the evil from this shrine.'

Thoas suspected nothing, and readily believed what she said. So while he remained to purify the shrine, Iphigenia, holding the image, led the way to the shore, Orestes and Pylades following with a guard of Taurians.

But when they reached the sea, the fifty Argives were waiting for them, and easily overcame the Tauric guard. Swiftly, then, they all entered the ship and sailed triumphantly away.

They came after an easy voyage to Greece, and there by command of Athena, the image of Artemis was set up in a temple near Athens, and Iphigenia continued to be its chief priestess. But never again was human sacrifice offered to it.

Orestes and Pylades reached Mycenae in safety, and there Orestes married Hermione: when Menelaus died they became King and Queen of Sparta as well, and both lived happily into old age.

Electra married Pylades, and they reigned happily in Phocis, when King Strophius died, and had three sons who were firm allies of King Tisamenes, the son of Orestes and Hermione.

CHAPTER 13

THE ADVENTURES OF MENELAUS

*

Helen, thy beauty is to me
    Like those Nicaean barks of yore,
That gently, o'er a perfumed sea,
    The weary, wayworn wanderer bore
To his own native shore.

EDGAR ALLAN POE
To Helen

CHAPTER THIRTEEN

WHEN the Greeks sailed away from Troy they did not all sail at the same time or in the same direction, so that various fortunes attended each of them. Menelaus and the majority of the Greek kings sailed later than Agamemnon, Diomedes and Nestor, and were scattered by a great storm.

Many of the ships were wrecked on the coast of Greece: for King Nauplius, in revenge for the death of his son Palamedes, lit false beacon lights on the rocky coast of Euboea, and the pilots believed them to mark the entrance to a harbour and steered their ships on to the rocks.

Neoptolemus with his followers landed safely in the north of Greece, and instead of returning home marched inland and conquered Molossia. Here he reigned for seven years, with Andromache as his queen; and they had a son called Molossus to succeed them. But at the end of this time Neoptolemus grew tired of Andromache and set out for Sparta to claim Hermione as his wife. On the way he visited Delphi, and not receiving the answer he wanted from the oracle, plundered the temple and burnt the shrine. When he reached Sparta Neoptolemus carried off Hermione, for at this time Orestes was still being pursued by the Furies during his year of exile. But returning by Delphi, Neoptolemus met Orestes who had come to consult the oracle: Neoptolemus was killed on the spot and buried under the temple which he had destroyed, and Hermione returned in safety to Sparta.

When the storm scattered the ships, Menelaus actually reached Greece and anchored at Sunium near Athens. But when he tried to sail across the Gulf of Aegina to reach Argos or some port near Sparta, the storm sprang up again and drove him south to the island of Crete.

After wandering about for some time he came to Cyprus, where he met one of the Greek heroes who had failed to reach home after the fall of Troy: Demophon the son of Theseus.

This prince does not seem to have tried very hard to reach Athens, for when he landed in Thrace on his way home, he fell in love with the Princess Phyllis. So he stayed there, married her and became king. But after a while he grew tired of Thrace and told Phyllis that he must leave her for a few months while he sailed down to Athens on a visit to his mother whom he had not seen for eleven years.

'It is not lawful for the King of Thrace to leave his country,' objected Phyllis. But Demophon pointed out that he was only king by right of his marriage to her, and that *she* must remain where she was.

'But I will not be away longer than three months,' said Demophon, and he swore the most solemn oaths by every one of the Immortals that he would be back in well under a year.

Phyllis bade farewell to him as he entered his ship, and gave him a little golden casket.

'This contains a charm,' she said. 'Open it a year from now if you have not returned by then.'

Demophon promised to do this, and set sail from Thrace. But he made no attempt to visit Athens; instead he steered straight for the island of Cyprus, and settled there.

He did not keep one of his oaths, but on the appointed day he opened the casket. At that very moment in far-away Thrace poor, deserted Phyllis died of a broken heart, and the Immortals turned her into an almond tree. But Demophon saw something in the casket which drove him mad on the spot. Leaping on a horse, he galloped screaming towards the sea-shore, his drawn sword in his hand; suddenly his horse stumbled, the sword flew from his hand and Demophon fell upon it and was killed instantly.

As he did so, the bare almond tree in Thrace blossomed into green leaves: and ever after that the Greeks called the new green leaves '*phylla*' after the faithful Princess Phyllis of Thrace.

Menelaus buried the body of Demophon, and set sail from Cyprus. But once again ill fortune befell him, and his ships were scattered in a storm. This time it was much worse than before, since Menelaus was washed overboard; and although he was safely picked up by another of his ships, when the storm ended there was no sign of the royal ship in which Helen was sailing.

Menelaus was in despair: to have sacked Troy for Helen's sake and then to lose her on the way home!

He searched for her up and down the Mediterranean, visiting various places in Africa, Asia Minor and Phoenicia, in vain. At last after several years, during which, though he had not found Helen he had collected much treasure, Menelaus came to the island of Pharos, one day's voyage from Egypt. There he landed with the four ships that remained to him, to rest before attempting the voyage home to Greece: for by now he had given up all hope of finding Helen.

But having landed on Pharos, he could not get away. The wind blew steadily from the north – and Menelaus knew that any strangers visiting Egypt were liable to find themselves made into slaves or even sacrificed by King Theoclymenus. Day after day the Greeks remained on Pharos; soon their food ran short, and they were driven to spending all their time catching fish to keep themselves from starving.

At length one day as Menelaus walked by himself on a lonely stretch of the shore, praying to the Immortals for aid, there came up out of the sea the nymph Idothea.

'You are very foolish and feeble-witted, Greek stranger!' she exclaimed. 'Or is it that you and your companions like sitting about on this desert island catching fish?'

Then Menelaus answered: 'Fair nymph, goddess or Immortal, who ever you may be: I do not

stay here of my own will, but because we cannot
get away. Therefore I beg you to tell me what I
must do to escape from this place: for surely the
Immortals hold me here because I have neglected
some honour which is their due.'

'That I do not know,' said Idothea, 'but my
father Proteus, the Old Man of the Sea, can read
both the past and the future. If you can catch and
hold him, he will tell you. But he is hard to catch
and harder still to hold. Yet I will help you, if you
will choose your three best men to accompany you,
and meet me here at daybreak tomorrow.'

Menelaus promised readily, and Idothea slipped
back into the sea. But she was waiting for them
next morning, carrying with her four newly-flayed
sealskins.

'You must dig yourselves holes here in the sand,'
she said, 'and I will cover you with the skins. For
at noon the Old Man of the Sea comes out of the
waves to sleep here on the shore, and with him
comes a great flock of seals to sleep also, and to
guard him. He will first number them as a shepherd does with his sheep, and then slumber in their
midst. When he is asleep, you four must spring out
of hiding and catch hold of him. By his magic he
will turn himself into all manner of creeping crea-
tures, and maybe into fire and water as well; but
if you can hold him tight, in the end he will return
to his own shape, and you may ask him what you
will, and he will return a true answer.'

So saying Idothea covered them with the sealskins and left them there; nor did they pass a very

pleasant morning, for the skins above them stank in the hot sun.

But at last the seals began to arrive and stretch themselves out to sleep on the sunny sands; and

Proteus woke and turned himself into a fierce lion

when they were all assembled Proteus came himself, the Old Man of the Sea, and counted his fishy flocks just as Idothea had said. When he was satisfied that all was well, he laid himself down to rest in their midst, not far from where Menelaus and his three companions were concealed.

As soon as he was asleep they sprang out and seized hold of him. At once Proteus woke and in a moment turned himself into a fierce lion, and after that into a snake, a leopard and a great wild boar. Still the four Greeks clung to him, and he turned himself into running water, and then into a tall tree. But, seeing that he could not shake them off, he returned to his own strange blue shape, and said:

'Hmm! Menelaus of Sparta! Doubtless some Immortal has told you how to catch me!'

'Old Man of the Sea, replied Menelaus, 'you know everything: so why ask me these vain questions?'

'Hmm! Exactly!' grunted Proteus, a merry twinkle in his bright blue eyes. 'You want to know why you are kept on this desert island? Yes, of course. Well, all you've to do is to fit out one ship and sail in her to Egypt. You've a sacrifice to offer there – and what is fated to happen, will happen! Hmm! Yes. And you'll get safely back to Greece as soon as you've done that, with four ships. You'll find that Agamemnon has been murdered by Aegisthus and Clytemnestra; and unless you hurry, Orestes will have avenged him by the time you land at Nauplia . . . You want to know about any-one else? Old Nestor got home first: you'll see him. Calchas met a prophet cleverer than himself, and died of fury . . . You said "How sad?" No, I thought not! . . . Odysseus? He's a prisoner on Calypso's enchanted isle. But he'll get back to Ithaca after ten years, it's all arranged up in Olympus . . . You and Helen? Oh yes, you'll live happily ever afterwards in Sparta, and you won't die, either. The Immortals will carry you both to the Elysian Fields which are at the world's end . . . That's all I can tell you . . . Now off you go to Egypt . . . Hurry!'

With that Proteus winked knowingly, and jumped backwards into the sea before they could prevent him.

However Menelaus knew enough now, and deciding to trust Proteus implicitly, he launched one of his ships and set sail for Egypt. The north wind blew steadily, so that the voyage was easy: but when they drew near to the mouth of the Nile, the wind increased suddenly to a gale, and dashed the ship to pieces on a reef of hidden rocks.

Menelaus and most of his men swam to the shore, and took shelter in a cave, drenched and miserable.

In the morning Menelaus set out alone, still encrusted with sea salt and grime, and perfectly disguised by the miserable raggedness to which the rocks had reduced all his fine clothes.

When he reached the city he was directed to the Temple of the Strange Hathor, where wanderers might find shelter, and reaching it he knelt down at the altar in the courtyard.

There the greatest surprise of all his adventures befell him: for presently the Priestess of Hathor came forward to the altar, and it was none other than Helen herself, attended by her four hand-maidens.

Very quickly Menelaus made himself known to

her, and Helen was filled with joy. But fear came very quickly on the heels of joy.

'If you are discovered, they will kill you!' she cried. 'And my death is near me also. For Theoclymenus, Egypt's King, comes this day to make me his wife by force. When the ship brought me here, his father the king who has recently died called me the Strange Hathor and made me Priestess of Hathor, which is their name for Aphrodite, here in this temple.

'But Theoclymenus is of another spirit and cares little for what we think right and wrong. Priestess though I am, he will make me his wife: all that troubles him is the thought that you, my husband, may still be alive.'

Then, their wits sharpened by the danger, they thought of a scheme to outwit Theoclymenus and win safely away, though the ship in which Menelaus came to Egypt had been dashed to pieces.

When Theoclymenus came to the Temple later that morning, Menelaus, still in his rags, knelt at the king's feet and cried:

'My lord, I bring news! Menelaus, King of Sparta, is dead! His ship was wrecked on your coast and I alone escaped from the angry sea and the sharp rocks. But Menelaus was killed: I saw with my own eyes how the rocks crushed his bones before the waves carried his body out to sea!'

Theoclymenus was delighted with this news, and turned to Helen exclaiming: 'Now there is nothing to keep us apart!'

'Nothing indeed,' sobbed Helen, 'and I will

marry you of my own wish and with full consent. But first grant me a request. Menelaus was a great king, and I loved him once: let me celebrate his funeral rites after the true Greek style.'

'Certainly you may,' said Theoclymenus, 'all that I have is yours. Do as you please, for I know not the funeral customs of the Greeks.'

'Then we must have a ship,' said Helen, 'for the rites of those lost at sea must be performed on the sea itself, at a spot where the land is only just in sight. I must have a bull to sacrifice: this ship-wrecked sailor can come and attend to that, since he is a Greek and knows well what to do. Then my Menelaus was a warrior, so I must have a fine suit of armour to cast into the sea in his honour. And there must be garments and ornaments too: and an offering of wine and bread . . .'

'All shall be as you desire,' said Theoclymenus. 'A ship of mine, manned by enough of my sailors to row or sail it shall be ready in an hour, and this Greek, since he is to perform the ceremony, shall be in command of it.'

So all things were prepared: Helen led the way, followed by her handmaidens who carried rich robes, jewels and other offerings, and Menelaus followed. On the quayside his own sailors who had survived the shipwreck joined them, since the bull proved difficult and could not be placed on board without their aid.

The ship set sail, and the wind blew suddenly from the south until soon the land grew dim behind them.

'Now for the sacrifice!' cried Menelaus, and slew the bull in fine style. 'And now,' he added, 'let us cast these Egyptian barbarians into the sea, to swim back to King Theoclymenus if they can, while we sail for Hellas!'

The Egyptians were soon overpowered, and, being good swimmers, most of them reached the shore to tell Theoclymenus how Menelaus had tricked him. But Menelaus himself sailed triumphantly away, was joined by his three ships as he passed the island of Pharos and came safely to Greece without any further adventures.

They landed at Nauplia, to find that Orestes had just killed Aegisthus and Clytemnestra and was about to be stoned by the people. But Apollo appeared at the right moment to save Hermione, whom Orestes and Electra had captured as a hostage, and when Orestes set out on his wanderings, Helen and Menelaus took their daughter back to Sparta to await his return.

When Neoptolemus came and carried her off, Menelaus prepared to set out in pursuit of them. But news came that the wicked son of Achilles had perished miserably at Delphi, and Hermione was on her way back to them, safe and unhurt.

A year later Orestes returned, his madness cured and his deeds forgiven and purified, and his wedding with Hermione was celebrated with all joy and honour.

Not long after they had gone to claim their kingdom at Mycenae, and ten years since the fall of Troy, a stranger prince arrived at Sparta. He was welcomed by kindly Menelaus, and that evening as he sat feasting in the great hall of the palace, Helen came forth from her fragrant chamber as bright as golden Artemis and still the loveliest woman in all the world, and greeted the young prince.

'Noble sir, none have I ever seen so like another, man or woman, as you are like one of the noblest of the Greeks, who suffered many things and did deeds unforgettable at Troy for my poor sake. Surely you must be Telemachus, the son whom Odysseus left as a new-born child in his palace when first he sailed for Troy?'

Then the stranger answered: 'Queen of Sparta, I am indeed Telemachus, the son of Odysseus. It is ten years since Troy fell, and he alone of all the heroes who fought there has not returned home: yet no news has come to us of his death.'

Then Helen and Menelaus welcomed Telemachus as warmly as if he had been their own son, and he told them how the palace at Ithaca was filled with evil men who were the suitors of Queen Penelope urging her to marry one of them and declaring that Odysseus was surely dead.

'He is not dead, and he will return this very year!' cried Menelaus. 'For so Proteus, the Old Man of the Sea, told me. Odysseus, he said, was held prisoner by the nymph Calypso in her magic isle, but would return to Ithaca ten years after the fall of Troy!'

CHAPTER 14

THE WANDERINGS OF ODYSSEUS

*

> Yet endure! We shall not be shaken
>   By things worse than these;
> We have 'scaped when our friends were taken,
>   On the unsailed seas
> Worse deaths have we faced and fled from,
>   In the Cyclops' den,
> When the floor of his cave ran red from
>   The blood of men.

ANDREW LANG
The World's Desire

CHAPTER FOURTEEN

WHEN the great storm scattered the Greek fleet as it sailed away from Troy, Odysseus and his twelve ships were driven northwards to Ismarus, a town in Thrace. They landed there and took the town by storm: for the Thracians were allies of the Trojans, and they knew that Odysseus had killed their king, Rhesus.

Odysseus however took care that no harm was done to Maron the priest of Apollo, and in gratitude Maron gave him twelve jars of wine so strong that each needed to be mixed with twenty times the quantity of water for a man to drink of it without intoxication.

Soon the Thracians from further inland came to attack Odysseus, and he put to sea as the lesser of two evils. The storm wind had veered round by now, and it drove him south for ten days and nights until he came to the land of the Lotus-eaters. Now whoever eats of the Lotus fruit forgets his home and all worthy things, desiring only to lie in the warm, sunny meadows and eat the Lotus for the rest of his life.

Odysseus sent some of his men to see who dwelt in that land; and these, when they had tasted the Lotus, forgot even to come back and tell him. So he set out with another party, found them and forced them back to the ships in spite of their prayers and lamentations. Then they sailed on,

and came to a big, fertile island on which grazed
many sheep. Cautious Odysseus left his fleet behind a rocky islet nearby and landed on the main
island with twelve men, leaving one ship with
the rest of its crew ready to sail at a moment's
notice.

Up the beach went Odysseus and his twelve
companions, and presently they came to a big cave
in which were jars of milk, big cheeses and huge
piles of firewood, besides many kids and lambs
playing in their wattle pens.

'Some shepherd must live here,' said Odysseus,
'and shepherds are usually friendly people. Let us
wait until he returns, and see if we can buy cheeses
and other stores from him.'

Evening seemed slow in coming, and while they
waited the men lit a fire and helped themselves to
some of the cheeses for their supper.

Then suddenly the owner of the cave arrived,
driving his flocks before him and carrying a dead
tree over one shoulder. Odysseus and his companions fled to the very back of the cave and hid
there, quaking in terror: for he was a terrible
Cyclops, a giant with only one eye which was in
the middle of his forehead.

When the Cyclops, whose name was Polyphemus, had milked his goats and ewes, he heaped
wood on to the fire, and the light revealed the men
hiding in the darkest corners.

'Ho-ho!' cried Polyphemus in a great voice.
'Who are you? Pirates, sea-robbers come to bring
ill upon other men and other men's goods?'

'Not so, mighty sir,' answered Odysseus, overcoming his fear with difficulty. 'We are poor Greeks returning from the sack of Troy, seeking our homes after many years of war. I beg you to deal kindly with us: for Zeus brings evil upon those who harm a stranger.'

Polyphemus laughed cruelly. 'Mad or foolish you must be, stranger,' he cried. 'For no Cyclops pays any heed to Zeus, nor indeed to any of the Immortals, save only Poseidon, ruler of the sea, for he is my father. But tell me, where did you leave your ship? In some safe bay of the island, I hope.'

Then Odysseus, fearing the worst, spoke words of guile. 'Alas,' he said, 'Poseidon who shakes the earth broke our tall ship to pieces on the rocks, and we poor few escaped only with our lives.'

Hearing this, the Cyclops growled angrily, and reaching out his great hand he seized two of the sailors in it, dashed out their brains on the rocky floor, cut them up and devoured them for his supper, even crunching up the bones with his strong teeth. Then he drank several vats of milk, and grunting happily, settled down on the floor and fell fast asleep.

Now Odysseus was minded to see if with a careful sword-stroke straight to the heart he could kill the monster as he slept. But he realized in time that to do so would mean their certain death since Polyphemus had placed across the doorway of the cave a mass of rock so huge that twenty men could not have stirred it.

In the morning Polyphemus awoke, milked his flocks, ate two more men and went out for the day blocking the cavemouth carefully behind him.

Then Odysseus set to work with the help of his terrified companions. He cut a great stake like the top of a mast, sharpened one end and hardened the point in the fire. Scarcely was this done and the weapon concealed under a pile of dung, when back came Polyphemus driving his sheep and goats before him. As on the previous evening he began by replacing the great stone over the cavemouth; then he attended to his flocks; and after that made his supper on two more of the companions of Odysseus.

When his meal was complete and he was just settling down for a good drink of milk before going to sleep, Odysseus stepped forward and bowing low held up a great wooden goblet filled with red wine: for by great good fortune he had brought with him one of the jars of strong wine which grateful Maron had given to him in Thrace.

'Cyclops, take and drink wine after your feast of man's flesh, so that you may know what sort of cargo our good ship held,' he said politely.

Polyphemus grabbed the cup and drained it at a gulp; then, smacking his lips, he handed it back to Odysseus demanding more: for he had never tasted wine.

'Fill again,' he hiccoughed, 'and then maybe I will give you a gift. For never have I drunk anything so good.'

Odysseus filled the cup yet again, and the Cyclops began to grow very intoxicated.

'Tell me your name, stranger,' he said. 'Then I can drink to your health.'

'Noble sir,' answered Odysseus, 'my name is Nobody. That's what my father and mother and my dear wife, and all my friends call me.'

'All right, Nobody,' grunted the Cyclops, 'this is my gift to you in exchange for the delicious drink – I'll eat you last of all your companions!'

And with that he sank down on the cave floor and fell fast asleep, snoring like a whole herd of swine.

Then Odysseus and his companions took the sharpened stake, and having made the end hot in the fire, they plunged it into the single eye of Polyphemus and twirled it round until he was blinded.

Polyphemus let out the most fearful yells and tried in vain to catch Odysseus and the rest of the men. Presently, hearing his cries, one Cyclops after another came running from their caves nearby to see what had happened.

'Polyphemus!' they called. 'Whatever makes you yell like that in the middle of the night? Surely no one is driving off your flocks; and even more surely you are not being slain by force or craft?'

Then Polyphemus shouted back from within the cave: 'Nobody is slaying me by guile! Nobody is slaying me by force!'

'Oh, if nobody is hurting you,' they answered crossly, 'you must be suffering from some pain sent by an Immortal. So pray to your father Poseidon, and let us get some sleep!'

Then they returned to their own caves, and Odysseus laughed to himself at the ease with which he had beguiled each foolish Cyclops.

Morning came, and Polyphemus opened the cave, since the sheep and goats had all to go out and graze. But he seated himself at the cave-mouth and felt each sheep as it passed him to make sure that the Greeks did not escape. But Odysseus tied the sheep together in sets of three, and under the middle sheep of each three he bound one of his men. Then he himself seized hold of the greatest ram in the flock and hung on to the thick wool under its belly.

'Alas my poor ram!' said Polyphemus as he stroked its back. 'Usually you run frisking to the pasture before any of the ewes. But today you linger behind: maybe you are sorry for your poor master whom this accursed Nobody has blinded!'

When they were clear of the cave, Odysseus released his companions and they hastened down to the ship, driving with them many of the sheep and goats.

As the ship sailed out from the land Odysseus stood in the stern and shouted aloud:

'Cyclops! You have not been cheated and blinded by a mere Nobody! If anyone asks who robbed you of your eye, you may tell him that it was Odysseus the sacker of cities, the son of Laertes, King of Ithaca!'

Polyphemus flung a mighty rock which almost hit the ship; but his second throw raised a great wave which washed it well out of his reach. Then he prayed to his Immortal father:

'Poseidon, girdler of the earth, grant that Odysseus the son of Laertes may never win home to Ithaca! But if it is ordained that he must return, then may he come late and in an evil plight; may he come in the ship of strangers, having lost all his companions, and may he find sorrows waiting for him in his home!'

Over the dancing waves sailed Odysseus, and he might have won home in spite of the Cyclops's curse had it not been for the greed and stupidity of his own men. For he came next to the Isle of the Winds, and there King Aeolus who held the winds in charge to loose or bind at the will of Zeus gave them all to Odysseus in a great oxhide bag. So they sailed peacefully home until they could see the very smoke rising from the chimneys in Ithaca. But then Odysseus, feeling that they were safe at last, fell asleep and his men opened the bag because they thought that it contained gold which he was keeping for himself. Out rushed the winds, and drove them back into unknown seas, and King Aeolus would not bind them again for Odysseus, who had missed his chance.

Now the curse of Polyphemus began to work upon them, for they were driven far across the sea and landed in the country of the Laestrygonians who were fierce cannibals. These people dropped huge rocks from the cliffs that sank all but one of the ships, and then caught the wretched sailors as they swam ashore.

Odysseus escaped in his own ship by cutting the cable, and they came sadly to the island of Aeaea where dwelt Circe the enchantress, the sister of Aeetes the king of Colchis whom Jason and Medea had visited many years before.

Not knowing what sort of entertainment to expect, Odysseus divided his company into half and cast lots as to which should go first to the buildings which they saw among the trees in the distance.

The lot fell on Eurylochus, who set out with his two and twenty companions, and came to a fair palace where Circe welcomed them kindly. All entered except Eurylochus who hid in the wood to see what would happen. Circe led the men to a table in the long hall and set before each of them a great bowl filled with cheese and honey and barley meal and wine: but with each there was mixed also a magic drug. When the men had drunk, she touched them with her wand, and at once they were all changed into swine which she drove out of the palace and shut up in a sty at the back.

Eurylochus returned with his terrible news, and Odysseus set out to punish Circe and try to restore his companions. As he walked through the wood Hermes the Immortal Messenger met him:

'Odysseus, you may not overcome Circe by your own strength and cunning,' said Hermes. 'But take this herb which is called "moly" and cast it, unseen, into the cup which she will mix for you. Then drink it without fear, and when she strikes you with her wand, draw your sword and threaten to slay her unless she restores your companions and vows to do no further harm to any of you. Then you must live here with her for a year, and she will make you her lord and the master of this island. But at the end of that time I will come again and see to it that she sends you on your way with all things needful for your voyage.'

All fell out as Hermes had said: the magic swine were restored to their human shapes, and Odysseus and his men passed a pleasant year in the enchanted palace of Circe.

At the end of that time the enchantress sent Odysseus on his way with his ship well-stored, but advised him first to seek guidance from the blind prophet Tiresias.

'He is numbered with the dead,' Circe told him, 'but you may come to the verge of the Realm of Hades by way of the Ocean Stream, the magic flood that girdles all the earth. Beach your ship where Acheron flows into Cocytus, a branch of the River Styx, and both run by a great rock into Ocean. There dig a trench, and pour forth the offerings, and the spirits of the dead will draw near to you. But keep them from the trench until Tiresias comes and you have learnt from him all that you need to know.'

Away sailed Odysseus from the fair Aeaean isle and came to the White Rock and the Poplars of Persephone. There he did as Circe had instructed

him, and learnt many things from the ghost of
Tiresias. There also he saw the spirits of many a
famous Hero and Heroine: his own mother, whom
he did not know had died, was the first to greet
him, and after her came Alcmena and Leda with
many others who had been the brides of Immortals.
He saw also the ghost of Agamemnon and learnt
of his miserable end; and he saw Achilles and the
other Heroes who had fallen at Troy: but when
Ajax came he would not greet Odysseus, being
still angered over their quarrel concerning the
armour of Achilles. Heracles came also, and many
more: yet these were but shadows, for Heracles
himself dwelt among the Immortals, and Achilles
walked the Elysian Fields with the dead Heroes.

Then Odysseus sailed away, back to the world
of light, and presently drew near to the island
where the two Sirens still dwelt, though the
rest of their number had perished when Jason
passed by them unscathed thanks to the song of
Orpheus.

Now when the ship drew near Odysseus instructed his men to bind him to the mast and not
to release him until the danger was passed. But to
the men themselves he gave lumps of wax which
they put into their ears so that they might not hear
the fatal singing.

On they sailed, and the Sirens sang their wonderful song, so that Odysseus forgot even his
wisdom at the sound, and shouted to his men to
unbind him. But they only bound him the tighter,
and rowed on with great strokes of their oars.

Odysseus instructed his men to bind him to the mast

Then the Sirens sang again in their irresistible voices:

'Come hither, hither over the wave,
Glory of Greece – Odysseus brave,
 And hark to our magic song.
For none has passed us over the main
Till he harkened the honey-sweet voice of us twain,
 And tested what joys belong
To the Siren maids: for all things we know,
Past, to come, and the end of woe
 In the bliss of our magic song!'

Odysseus shouted and struggled until he was

exhausted, and when the Sirens' Isle was left far behind his men released him and drew the wax from their ears.

Thus Odysseus was the only man who ever heard the Sirens singing and lived to tell of their song: for the music of Orpheus had drowned their singing when the Argonauts passed by. But the two Sirens fell from their rocks and died: for this doom was decreed if once a mortal escaped them after he had heard their song.

The next danger came to Odysseus as his ship sped between Italy and Sicily: for on one side of the straits was the great whirlpool of Charybdis, and on the other the sea-dragon Scylla lurked in her cave. Remembering Circe's advice, Odysseus steered well away from Charybdis: but just as they swept by, Scylla appeared at her cave-mouth and grabbed six men with her octopus-like tentacles. While she was feasting on these, the ship passed into safety, and they anchored at Trinacria, an island of the Sun.

Here grazed the golden cattle of the Sun Titan Helios, which Tiresias had warned Odysseus not to touch. Odysseus passed the warning on to his men. But after they had been becalmed there for many days, and were growing hungry, they disobeyed his orders and killed several of the cattle on which they feasted for six days.

The wind rose on the seventh and they sailed away: but Helios had reported the theft to Zeus who hurled a thunderbolt which split the ship and drowned all save Odysseus who clung to the mast

and floated away. He could not steer, and saw
with terror that he was drifting towards the whirlpool of Charybdis. Into the whirlpool went the
mast and was sucked down: but Odysseus leapt
from it just in time and caught hold of a wild fig-
tree which grew from the cliff above. To this he
clung until he saw the mast shot up from the depths
by the whirlpool: then he cast himself on to it, and
was washed away until, nearly dead from exhaus-
tion, the mast came to land on the island of Ogygia.

In this magic isle dwelt the nymph Calypso,
daughter of the Titan Atlas. She welcomed Odysseus, tended and fed him and begged him to remain with her for ever.

'I will make you immortal,' she said, 'for indeed
on this magic isle old age does not come. Here we
may live for ever, the King and Queen of fair
Ogygia, and you will have no more troubles, for
suffering and sorrow shall be far from you.'

But Odysseus, faithful to his home and longing
for his wife Penelope, refused to wed Calypso or
to vow to remain with her for ever. But he could
not escape since his ship was lost and she would
allow him no tools with which to build a new one.
And she kept him there for seven long years while
he sat day after day on the sea-shore gazing across
the blue waves towards distant Ithaca and weary-
ing his heart with longing.

At length Athena, who took special care of
Odysseus, went to Olympus and begged Zeus to
grant him a safe home-coming.

'My heart is torn for wise Odysseus, that hapless

one,' she said. 'It is ten years since Troy was taken and still he alone of heroes has not won to his home. But now the guileful daughter of Atlas keeps him for the seventh year in her sea-girt isle striving to make him forget Ithaca: but Odysseus, yearning to see if it were but the smoke rise upwards from his own land, desires else to die.'

Then Zeus made answer to wise-eyed Athena:

'My daughter, I have not forgotten the much enduring Odysseus whom Poseidon, girdler of the earth, keeps from home in his anger at the blinding of his Cyclops son Polyphemus whose mother was Thoosa child of the Sea Titan giant Phorcus. And now I will send Hermes the Messenger to Ogygia: for the time approaches when Odysseus shall come home.'

So Hermes came to Calypso and told her the commands of Zeus: and she, weeping sorely, gave Odysseus all the tools that he needed to construct a big raft, and stores of wine, grain and dried flesh to take when it was made.

Then she bade him farewell and he sailed over the smooth sea with a glad heart. But Poseidon, returning to Olympus from the land of the Ethiopians, and not knowing the will of Zeus, saw Odysseus nearing the land of Phaeacia on his raft. Then in a fury Poseidon called up the stormwinds, and whirling Odysseus into the deep, went on his way well pleased, deeming that this was the end.

But Odysseus came safely to shore, and was found by the Princess Nausicaa who brought him

to her father the King of Phaeacia, who entertained him kindly, listened to all his story and at
length sent him home to Ithaca in one of his own
ships.

As it sped over the sea Odysseus fell into a deep
sleep, and the kindly Phaeacians landed him still
sleeping and left him under a tree, surrounded
with rich and generous gifts: and thus after ten
years of wandering, Odysseus came home.

CHAPTER 15

ODYSSEUS IN ITHACA

*

Penelope for her Ulysses' sake
   Devised a Web her wooers to deceive
In which the work that she all day did make
   The same at night she did again unreave.

SPENSER
Sonnet xxiii

CHAPTER FIFTEEN

WHEN Odysseus awoke from sleep a mist lay over all the place and he did not know where he was. At first he lamented, thinking that the Phaeacians had landed him on some desert island and left him to his fate. But presently Athena came to him and drew back the mist. Then Odysseus knew his home, and kneeling down kissed the soil of Ithaca in his joy and thankfulness.

'There is still much trouble before you,' Athena warned him. 'For a hundred and eight suitors have gathered in your hall to woo your wife Penelope. They dwell in the town, but come each day and feast riotously on your possessions: your flocks and herds grow few, your wine is well-nigh exhausted. But still your faithful Penelope holds them at bay, though she nears the end of her strength.'

Then Athena told Odysseus how Penelope had baulked the suitors for three years with a cunning almost equal to his own.

'I cannot choose a husband,' Penelope had said, 'until I have woven a fine robe to be the winding shroud of the hero Laertes, father of my lord whom you say is dead. It must be a worthy robe, fit for a hero: alas that I could not weave one for my lord Odysseus!'

So Penelope wove at her loom day by day, working hard to make the shroud for Laertes; but every night she stole secretly to her loom and unravelled all that she had woven during the day. But at the end of three years some of her maids, who had fallen in love with several of the Suitors, betrayed her, and the Suitors lay in wait and caught her unpicking the web.

Then they came in a body and told her that she must make her choice without any more delay. Penelope begged for a few weeks in which to decide, and this they allowed.

'But today is her last day of grace,' ended Athena, 'and tomorrow they will demand her answer. It was when she knew that the end was near that she sent Telemachus to seek news of you. He is at Sparta, but I have been to him there, and he will return today. Go now to the cottage of Eumaeus the faithful swine-herd, whose father was a Prince of Phoenicia from whom he was stolen in childhood and sold as a slave to your father Laertes: him you may trust, and Philoetius the herdsman. But you must go in disguise . . .'

Athena spoke more words of advice to Odysseus, and helped him to make himself like an old beggar. After this she departed to guide Telemachus across the sea from Pylos to Ithaca in such a way as to avoid a band of Suitors who had laid an ambush for him between two islands: Athena came to Telemachus in the guise of his wise tutor Mentor, and brought him safely home that day.

Meanwhile Odysseus hid all the Phaeacian gifts in a cave, and trudged up the beach in his rags and came after a short walk to the cottage of

Eumaeus. Out rushed the dogs to drive off the beggar, and Odysseus sat down hastily, to show that he was a friend – a sign which Greek dogs still understand!

Eumaeus came forth, welcomed the beggar kindly into his cottage and fed him well, though he had no idea whom he was really entertaining. Odysseus did not reveal himself until Telemachus came; but then they rejoiced together and made their plans against the Suitors.

That evening Telemachus returned to the palace, and when the Suitors had gone home to bed, he removed all the weapons and armour which usually hung on the walls and pillars in the great hall where the feasts were held. He did not tell Penelope that Odysseus was in Ithaca, nor anything of the plan, but he suggested that, next day when the Suitors came to demand her hand in marriage for one of them, she should consent to marry whoever could bend the bow of Odysseus and shoot an arrow through the rings in the heads of twelve axes set up in a row – a feat which Odysseus himself had often performed in the days before he sailed to Troy.

Next morning Odysseus the beggar came up to the palace, and on the way he met Melanthius the goatherd who jeered at him and kicked him in the side, calling him vile names.

'If ever the great Odysseus returns,' said Eumaeus sternly, 'you will suffer for treating a stranger like this.'

'Oh, he'll never return,' cried Melanthius.

'Depend upon it, he lies dead in some foreign field – and I only wish Telemachus was as dead as he is!'

Odysseus passed on to the palace, and at the gate he saw his ancient hound Argus, blind and mangey, lying in the dirt where the Suitors had kicked him out to die. But as he drew near the old dog knew him, even after all those years: he struggled to his feet, sniffed at Odysseus, then licked his hand, whining with joy, and wagging his tail feebly – then sank down dead.

There were tears in his eyes as Odysseus stopped to stroke his old friend and lay him out gently by the palace wall.

Inside the courtyard Odysseus begged food from the Suitors, and was not kindly received. And there a real beggar called Irus tried to drive him out; for Irus was ravenously greedy, and spent all his time eating and drinking, and feared that the new beggar might take some of the food which would otherwise come to him.

Odysseus argued with him gently, but Irus would not be reasonable and challenged him to fight with fists. The Suitors gathered round laughing to watch the duel between the two beggars, and promised to see fair play and reward the winner.

When Odysseus bared his strong arms, Irus was afraid and would have slunk away; but the Suitors jeered at him and made him fight, calling him a bully and a cowardly braggart – as indeed he was.

So Irus rushed in with a yell and struck Odysseus on the shoulder, but Odysseus struck back, though not as strongly as he could have done, and stretched Irus bleeding on the ground. Then he dragged him out of the palace, propped him up against the wall and left him, saying:

'Sit there now, and scare off the swine and dogs; and do not bully beggars again, or a worse thing may befall you!'

Odysseus then returned to the palace, and Penelope sent for him since she had heard that he could give her news of the fall of Troy, and perhaps even of her lost husband.

Odysseus told her as much as seemed good for her to know at that moment, and when his tale was ended, Penelope bade the old nurse Euryclea wash his feet for him and find him some decent clothes to wear – for she knew that he spoke the truth and had really met her husband on his wanderings as he brought her a sure token.

As Euryclea washed his feet with warm water, she came to the scar from the wound which the boar had made on Mount Parnassus when Odysseus was a boy, and she recognized it and knew then who he was.

She would have cried out with joy, but Odysseus put his hand over her mouth quickly:

'Do you want to cause my death?' he whispered. 'If the Suitors know, they will murder me at once. Keep my return a secret, even from the Queen: the time will soon come when justice shall be done.'

After this he slipped back into the hall and waited quietly. Presently Penelope came in, fair and stately, carrying the great black bow and a quiverful of arrows. At her command twelve axes were set up in a line, and then she said:

'Princes and nobles, I can stand out against you no longer. Therefore whoever among you can string the bow of Odysseus and shoot an arrow through the rings in the axe-heads as he used to do, the same shall be my husband and the lord of rugged Ithaca, and Zacynthos and wooded Same.'

So the Suitors began in turn to handle the great bow; but not one of them could so much as string it. Then they grew angry, and declared that it was some trick of Penelope's, and that the bow could not be strung by any mortal man.

'Let me try,' said Odysseus, but the Suitors cried out at the impudence of the beggar, and one of them flung a stool at him.

'He shall try if he likes,' cried Telemachus, and it seemed as if a quarrel were about to begin. So he turned to Penelope and bade her go to her room with all her maidens; and when she had gone he sent Euryclea to lock them in. While this was happening Philoetius slipped into the courtyard and locked the gates also, that none might come out or in.

Then, at a word from Telemachus, Eumaeus picked up the bow and carried it to Odysseus. He took it in his hands, turning this way and that lovingly, testing it to see that all was well with it; then suddenly he bent it and slipped the string into place as easily as a minstrel strings his lyre. And beneath his fingers the bow-string sang like a swallow, yet with a deeper, fiercer note telling of war and of the death of men.

While the Suitors sat back in anger and amazement Odysseus set an arrow to the string, drew,

Odysseus set an arrow to the string

and loosed so surely that it sped through all twelve of the rings without touching one with its brazen barb.

'Telemachus, your guest does you no shame!' cried Odysseus, and with a bound he was on the high threshold with the arrows ready to his hand

and the beggar's rags cast from him. 'Lo, now is the terrible trial ended at last,' he continued, 'and I aim at another mark!'

Even as he spoke an arrow hummed from the bow, and one of the Suitors fell back dead in his seat, pierced through the throat.

'Mind where you're shooting!' shouted some of the Suitors, still not recognizing him and thinking that the last shot had been a mistake.

'That will I indeed,' was the answer, 'for you have much to answer, you who thought that I would never come back from the land of the Trojans, and therefore wasted my goods and insulted my wife. Now death waits for you, one and all, at the hand of Odysseus the sacker of cities!'

Then, while the great bow sang and the swift shafts hummed, the Suitors strove vainly to get at him and pull him down. First they sought for weapons, but these were not in the usual places on the walls. Then such as carried swords attacked him, using tables as shields; but Telemachus brought helmets, spears and shields for himself and faithful Eumaeus and Philoetius, and armour for Odysseus also, and the battle raged furiously.

Once it was almost lost, for false Melanthius the goatherd slipped into the store-room and brought out several weapons for the Suitors: but Telemachus caught him in time and tied him up, to be punished afterwards.

On and on shot Odysseus, and Athena spread panic among the Suitors so that they did not rush the four all in a single body as they might have done. When his arrows were exhausted, Odysseus took up the spears which had been flung at him and returned them to the Suitors with deadly aim; and drawing his sword he leapt among them, crying his terrible war-cry. At his side fought brave young Telemachus, and Eumaeus the faithful swineherd, and Philoetius the cowherd; and all of them were wounded in that terrible fray.

At length the Suitors lay dead, every man of them: but Odysseus spared Phemius the minstrel who had done no harm, and a slave who chanced to be in the hall and hid under an ox-hide.

Then Odysseus called for Euryclea, and she brought the handmaidens, and together they carried the bodies out of the palace, and cleansed the hall, and set all in order.

When this was done, Euryclea went to fetch Penelope who all the while had been sleeping peacefully in her inner chamber.

'Awake, dear child!' cried the old nurse. 'Awake and see the day for which you have prayed so long! For Odysseus has come – he is here in his own house, and has slain the proud Suitors who troubled you so and devoured all his substance!'

But Penelope would not believe the good news, not even when she came into the hall and found Odysseus waiting for her.

'I have heard it said,' she replied when Telemachus reproached her, 'that traitor Paris put on the form of Menelaus and so beguiled fair Helen my cousin. And well I know that the Immortals can wear what shape they will!'

Then Odysseus said to Telemachus: 'Son, your mother speaks wisely: for we have tokens that we twain know, secret from all others.'

Then Odysseus was bathed and clad in fair garments, and Penelope felt almost sure that he was indeed her husband. But still she doubted, and as a test she said:

'Noble sir, let us wait until tomorrow before we test one another further. But now I will command my maidens to bring forth the bed of Odysseus, whom you swear that you are – even his bridal bed and mine, which stands in the innermost chamber.'

Then Odysseus turned upon her, saying:

'This is a bitter word that you speak! Who has been interfering with my bed? For there is no man living, however strong, who could lift it and bring it here. And I will tell you why: when I married you, and built on our chamber to the palace, there stood an olive tree as thick as a pillar; round this I built the room, and roofed it over, but the lower branches of the tree I lopped off, and used the tree, still growing, as one of the corner posts of the bed. Lady, here is a token for you! I say that the bed cannot be brought out to me, unless some man has cut away the stem of the olive tree.'

When she heard this, Penelope's last doubt was gone. She broke into weeping, and ran up to him, cast her arms about his neck and kissed him, saying:

'Odysseus, my husband! None but you and I knew of the olive tree that is part of the bed in our secret bridal chamber. Now I know you indeed, and now I am truly happy once more!'

Then Odysseus held her in his arms; and in the happiness of that moment it seemed that all his toils and all his wanderings were but little things compared with so great and true a joy.

CHAPTER 16

THE LAST OF THE HEROES

*

... My purpose holds
To sail beyond the sunset, and the baths
Of all the western stars, until I die.
It may be that the gulfs will wash us down;
It may be we shall touch the Happy Isles.

TENNYSON
Ulysses

CHAPTER SIXTEEN

AND that is where the old tales come to an end, for Odysseus was really the last of the Heroes. There were no stories about Telemachus or his children: the old books say that he had a son called Perseptolis – but that is only because doubtless some Greek family claimed descent from him. In his lifetime the great grandsons of Heracles came back to Greece and conquered most of it – but that is where history begins and legend ends.

For the Heroic Age ended when Odysseus died: its brief, golden gleam lasted only a little while – the triple lifetime of Tiresias – and then the Immortals ceased to mingle visibly with mankind, and neither Zeus nor any of them married mortals nor had mortal children: Helen was the youngest child of Zeus.

When Homer wrote his two wonderful epic poems, *The Iliad* and *The Odyssey*, nearly three thousand years ago, he looked back less than two centuries to events which had already become legends, and wove them into immortal works which were the centre of all later poems and plays about the Immortals and the Heroes. All other tales of Troy fit into what Homer had already written.

The Tales end with Odysseus, but how did Odysseus end? The Greeks asked this question very early, and a poet made a short poem which is now lost. But what we know of it is very slight, and it was simply made to fit what Homer tells us.

For when Odysseus called up the ghost of Tiresias he received instructions as to his future course, and a veiled prophecy that, in his old age, death would come to him 'from the sea'.

When the Suitors were dead, their friends and relations wanted to kill Odysseus, and he was only saved by Athena who came from Zeus to make peace and send Odysseus on his last voyage to seek for the palace of sacrifice of which Tiresias had told him. So Odysseus set sail for the mainland, and when he reached the shore he went into the interior on foot, carrying an oar over his shoulder.

For weeks and weeks he went on, until at last he came to the land of the Thresprotians. And one day he passed two men working in a field, and one said to the other:

'Whatever is that stranger carrying on his shoulder?' And the other replied:

'It must be a winnowing fan for separating chaff from corn. I'm sure I can't think of any other use for it!'

Then Odysseus knew that he had reached a country where men had never heard of the salt sea, and thankfully he set the oar in the earth and offered the necessary sacrifice to Poseidon whom he had offended long ago when he blinded Polyphemus the Cyclops.

On his way home Odysseus tarried for a while with Queen Callidice and helped her to overcome the Brygians who were invading her country. Then

he returned home and lived happily with Penelope
and a son who was born to them after his return
from Troy called Poliporthes, while Telemachus
he made King of Ithaca.

But Odysseus had another son of whom he knew

*This wounded Odysseus, who never recovered, but fell
quietly asleep*

nothing. His name was Telegonus, and his mother
was Circe the enchantress.

When he was grown up, Telegonus set out to
seek for his father, and he sailed in vain to many
lands. At last a storm drove him to Ithaca, and he
landed without knowing where he was, and his

men killed some of the cattle and began to drive off the rest.

Then old Odysseus set out to chase away these thieves. But as Telegonus entered his ship he turned and flung a spear tipped with the poisonous spine of the sting-ray. And, as was decreed, this wounded Odysseus, who never recovered but fell quietly asleep.

Then the Immortals carried him away to the Elysian Fields at the World's End, there to live happily for ever with the other Heroes:

'No snow is there, nor yet great storm, nor any rain; but always ocean sendeth forth the breeze of the shrill West to blow cool – where life is easiest for men.'

ENVOI

Pass with a ringing laugh, a friendly word,
   Thinking of Rhintho resting here alone:
The Muses' smallest, least-remembered bird
   Plucked from their hill this garland of his own.

From the Greek of Nossis

AUTHOR'S NOTE

The Tale of Troy forms a natural sequel to *Tales of the Greek Heroes*, though the story is complete in itself. It is, indeed, the last great adventure of the Heroic Age, the culmination of the myths and legends which went before it, and the prelude to the real history of Greece – just as the *Iliad* and the *Odyssey*, the first and greatest surviving poems of ancient Greece, were the starting point for all later Greek literature.

The parts which make up the Tale of Troy have been told often before in one form or another, but usually as simple versions of the *Iliad* and the *Odyssey*, as by Charles Lamb in *The Adventures of Ulysses* or A. J. Church in *The Children's Iliad*. Books of stories from Greek myth and legend besides the tales from Homer occasionally include an incident or two from the rest of the Trojan cycle; and the story of the Wooden Horse makes a part of any re-telling of Virgil's *Aeneid*. But the whole tale has seldom been re-told: perhaps the most memorable version is that by Andrew Lang included fifty years ago in his *Tales of Troy and Greece*, though the account of the Trojan War is there told as the adventures of Odysseus, dwelling on his exploits and passing over much that is part of the story if taken as a whole.

Lang based his story on the obvious sources, the *Iliad*, the *Odyssey* and the *Posthomerica* of Quintus Smyrnaeus: but he admitted privately in a letter to his brother that he had not scrupled to invent where there were gaps in his originals.

The three epics have, naturally, been my main sources likewise, but I have refrained firmly from taking any liberties whatsoever with my authorities; and it chanced that I had not read Lang's version – and refrained from doing so until my own was written. As my story treats of the whole Adventure of Troy, I have cast my net far wider than Lang ever dreamed of doing – ranging from fragments and summaries of the lost Epic Cycle to the minor narrative poems of Colluthus and Tryphiodorus, from plays like the *Aias* or *Philoctetes* of Sophocles, the *Oresteia* of Aeschylus and a good ten by Euripides, to the death of Castor and Polydeuces as described by Theocritus or the tragedy of Corythus as sketched by Parthenius. But any full list of my authorities would be tedious and out of place. I want to say, however, that I have played fair with them: I hope that I have never falsified, and as far as I know I have not added a single incident, nor altered any legend, though I have sometimes omitted or toned down where desirable.

To this statement I must add a confession of my one and only conscious variation: I have suggested (without authority) that Helen became separated from Menelaus on the return from Troy, and so was able to be in Egypt before him. This allows the introduction of the adventures described by Euripides in his *Helena*, without having recourse to the 'eidolon' or double-Helen story invented by Stesichorus.

Apart from a reference to the medieval story of Troilus, I have otherwise full Classical authority for everything in this book. Indeed I have ancient Greek authority for all but the wanderings of Aeneas which, with a few minor details about the fall of Troy, are based on the *Aeneid*. I have sternly repressed the temptation to use that beautiful and moving romance *The World's Desire*, produced in 1890 by Rider Haggard and Andrew Lang as a sequel to the *Odyssey*, in place of the unsatisfactory summaries by Proclus and Apollodorus of the last adventures and death of Odysseus which are all that have come down to us. But I recommend that book to my readers.

At this date it is hardly necessary to make any remark about the use of the correct Greek names for the Gods and Heroes of Ancient Greece; I have added a list of the Greek and Roman equivalents. In deference to the general literary tradition I have used the Latinized spellings such as Phoebus Apollo for Phoibos Apollon and Circe for Kirke. I have used the Latin form, Ajax, for the son of Telamon merely to distinguish him from Aias the son of Oileus, and it has seemed better to retain such universally recognized variations as Priam, Hecuba and Helen for Priamos, Hekabe and Helena. But against Ulysses I have set my face firmly: he is as different from Odysseus as Jove and Juno are from Zeus and Hera. The Roman names are apt to suggest the artificial epic and the literary conventions of Virgil, Ovid and their tradition; the true Greek names fling wide the magic casements on the instant. Led by them we step directly back into the Heroic Age, into the bright, misty morning of legend and literature,

> *And hear, like ocean on a western beach,*
> *The surge and thunder of the Odyssey.*

ROGER LANCELYN GREEN

THE GODS AND GODDESSES OF ANCIENT GREECE

Greek	Latin
CRONOS	SATURN
RHEA	CYBELE
HELIOS	SOL (The Sun)
EOS	AURORA (The Dawn)
SELENE	LUNA (The Moon)
ZEUS	JUPITER or JOVE
POSEIDON	NEPTUNE
HADES	PLUTO or DIS
DEMETER	CERES
HESTIA	VESTA
HERA	JUNO
PERSEPHONE	PROSERPINE
ARES	MARS
DIONYSUS	BACCHUS
HERMES	MERCURY
HEPHAESTUS	VULCAN
ATHENA	MINERVA
ARTEMIS	DIANA
APHRODITE	VENUS
ASCLEPIUS	AESCULAPIUS
HERACLES	HERCULES or ALCIDES

APOLLO, PAN and HECATE are the same in both.

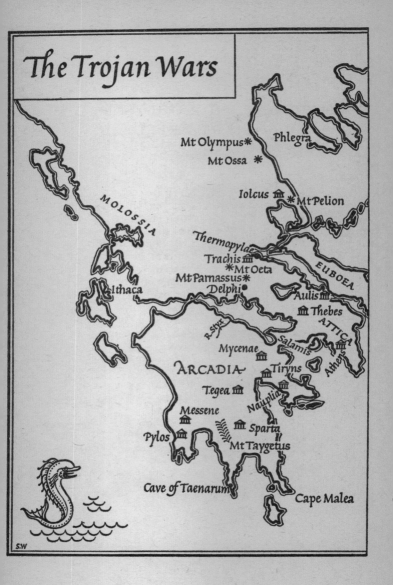

The Trojan Wars

Mt Olympus ✳ Phlegra
Mt Ossa ✳

Iolcus 🏛 ✳ Mt Pelion

MOLOSSIA

Thermopylae
Trachis 🏛 EUBOEA
✳ Mt Oeta
Mt Parnassus ✳
Delphi ● Aulis 🏛
Ithaca
🏛 Thebes
ATTICA

R. Styx
Mycenae 🏛 Salamis
ARCADIA Tiryns 🏛 Athens
Tegea 🏛
Nauplia
Messene 🏛
Pylos 🏛 ✳ Sparta
Mt Taygetus

Cave of Taenarum Cape Malea

S.W

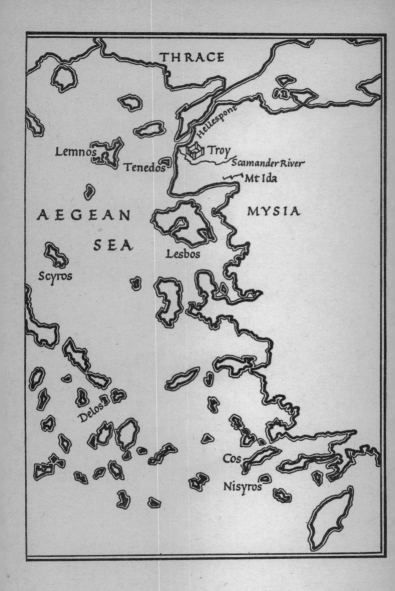

Also by Roger Lancelyn Green

THE ADVENTURES OF ROBIN HOOD

The tales of Robin Hood and his merry men in Sherwood Forest, which never cease to fire the imagination.

KING ARTHUR AND HIS KNIGHTS OF THE ROUND TABLE

The old stories of chivalry told afresh from the original sources, with beautiful scissor-cut pictures by Lotte Reiniger.

TALES OF THE GREEK HEROES

The author has re-told the legends as the Greeks themselves thought of them, as the history of the Heroic Age.

TALES OF ANCIENT EGYPT

This collection of the legends of Egypt will enrich the memory and brighten the imagination of everyone who enjoys myths and legends.

THE LUCK OF TROY

When Nicostratus was two he and his mother, the beautiful Helen, were carried off by Prince Paris of Troy. Ten years later he vows to help the Greek army to capture Troy.

Some other Puffins you might enjoy

I, JUAN DE PAREJA

Elizabeth Borton de Treviño

Juan was born into slavery early in the seventeenth century. He was orphaned when he was five years old, and when his mistress died of the plague she left him in her will to her nephew who lived in Madrid. This was Don Diego Rodriguez de Silva Velazquez, the painter, who treated him gently and saw that he was healed, washed, and given new clothes. So, given new faith by kindness, Juan grew into a loyal and devoted servant.

Only two things haunted him – the dread that he might be sold away into crueller slavery, and the law that forbade slaves to practise the arts. In a household that lived for painting, how could Juan resist the temptation to work secretly at what he loved best in the world?

I AM DAVID

Anne Holm

David lay quite still in the darkness of the concentration camp, waiting for the signal. 'You must get away tonight,' the man had told him. 'Stay awake so that you're ready just before the guard is changed. When you see me strike a match, the current will be cut off and you can climb over – you'll have half a minute, no more. Follow the compass southwards till you get to Salonica and then find a ship that's bound for Italy, and then go north till you come to a country called Denmark – you'll be safe there.'

So David, who had known no other life but that of the concentration camp, escaped into a world he knew nothing of, not even what things to eat nor how to tell good men from bad.

A deeply moving story, highly recommended for readers of 11 and over.

HORNED HELMET

Henry Treece

This is the story of Beorn, an Icelandic boy who runs away from a cruel master, is befriended by Starkad the fearful Baresark Jomsviking and joins his ship. As the Vikings make their swift deadly raids along the Scottish coast Beorn learns to fight, to kill, to sing their songs and to accept their rigid code. 'Jomsvikings are not concerned with manners, only with truth and hard-dealing. Never talk to a Jomsviking just for the sake of politeness. We have sworn an oath only to say what is so, no more and no less.'

There is no softness in this book. It is a magnificent saga of the Norsemen showing both their courage and brutality with a ring of truth.

DRAGON SLAYER

THE STORY OF BEOWULF

Rosemary Sutcliff

Lion-hearted Beowulf, the hero who had the strength of thirty men in his arms, sailed away over the whale road to rid the Danes of their deadly scourge, the prowling monster who struck terror into the bravest warriors of Denmark as they waited night after night in King Hrothgar's court. Great glory came to Beowulf before he died, the renown from his three great battles, with Grendel and his fearful mother, and with the dragon who guarded the brilliant treasure-hoard hidden away in the earth.

Rosemary Sutcliff's retelling of the Anglo-Saxon epic *Beowulf* grasps the splendour and mystery of the original poem. It is a story to feed the imagination powerfully, and fill the mind with a trembling awe.

EARTHFASTS

William Mayne

At the dusk of a summer's day, Keith Heseltine and David Wix were still out on Haw Bank, investigating something. There was a new mound in the grass, and it was getting bigger. Then the ground stirred, as if someone were getting out of bed. And with the movement came the sound of drumming. David was trembling all over, and so was Keith, and then they made sense of it. All that had come out of the hill was a boy about their own size, with a drum.

Two hundred years before, Nellie Jack John the drummer boy had gone to explore the passage under the castle, looking for King Arthur with his sleeping knights. Now he had come out again, but time had got mixed up, so that the ancient dead giants were walking about again, and domestic pigs were transformed into dangerous wild swine.

A BOOK OF HEROES

edited by William Mayne

Here are all sorts of heroes and all kinds of heroism, gathered together from all the corners of the globe. Some of the heroes are familiar. There is Orlando, whose exploits at the Battle of Roncesvalles were sung at the Battle of Hastings in 1066. There is a fleet of sea heroes – Sir Francis Drake, Sir Richard Grenville, John Paul Jones. But there are also many less well-known stories, like the one about Kagssagssuk, the homeless Eskimo boy who became so strong he could wring a bear's neck with his bare hands. Or the one about Volund the crippled smith tricking wicked King Nidud.

For readers of 8 to 12.

THE WHITE DRAGON

Richard Garnett

This is a bustling, cheerful story of a hard winter in the fens, and the doings of a group of lively teenagers in a small isolated community – skating, ice-sailing, telling ghost stories, amateur theatricals and archaeology, and of course unravelling the secret of the White Worme. It will have a special appeal for anyone who likes realistic stories which explain properly how things are made and done. For readers of 11 and over.

THE TWENTY-TWO LETTERS

Clive King

Long ago, 1500 years before Christ was born, when King Minos of Crete still worshipped the bull, when the Eastern Mediterranean was divided into many unstable little states, and Egyptian writing was a sacred and secret cult, Resh the master builder lived in the city of Byblos with his three sons and his daughter.

Resh was very busy building a new palace for the King, but his three sons went off in different directions. All the time they were away their father and sister Beth were waiting anxiously for their safe return with the presents they should give the King on his Day of Offering. But despite the unheard-of way Aleph sent a message warning the King of his enemies' approach, nothing could prevent the disaster which the strange men from the eastern land of Chaldea had foretold.

THE STORY OF JESUS

Eleanor Graham

The story is told realistically, from all four Gospels, with events as nearly as possible in chronological order. Through it comes a powerful feeling of purpose, and of a terrible campaign waged single-handed and to the death. It shows Jesus as, unquestionably, an historical figure, an unprivileged man but with the light of divinity shining through him.

He lived at a time and in a place we now know a good deal about from independent sources and archaeological discoveries; and modern translations have added new insights to the old text. Jesus himself left no documents or papers but many witnesses who had watched him heal, seen the feeding of the five thousand, and heard countless times his message, learned the Lord's Prayer from his lips, and passed it on so that it has come right down to our own generation.

There are many moving and dramatic pictures by Brian Wildsmith, which support the text magnificently.

HERO TALES FROM THE BRITISH ISLES

Barbara Leonie Picard

All the world worships a hero, and every part of Britain has its own legends about men of glorious valour and derring-do. In this collection you will find all the great names, from Cuchulain the champion warrior who single-handed defended Ulster against the whole army of Connaught, to Taliesin the Welsh boy who became a famous poet, prophet and magician.

There are plenty of rousing stories but the romantic ones are the most haunting. Deirdre's lament for her slain brothers, and the legend that Arthur and his knights lie sleeping in a cave until Britain needs them, have a poetry which will last forever.

If you have enjoyed this book and would like to know about others which we publish, why not join the Puffin Club? You will be sent the Club Magazine *Puffin Post* four times a year and a smart badge and membership book. You will also be able to enter all the competitions. Write for details to:

The Puffin Club Secretary
Penguin Books
Bath Road
Harmondsworth
Middlesex